ACCIDENTAL SINGLETON

ACCIDENTAL SINGLETON

The art of being single in midlife

KATE MULVEY

First published 2013 by
New Holland Publishers Pty Ltd
London • Sydney • Cape Town • Auckland

Garfield House 86–88 Edgware Road London W2 2EA United Kingdom
Wembley Square First Floor Solan Road Gardens Cape Town 8001 South Africa
1/66 Gibbes Street Chatswood NSW 2067 Australia
218 Lake Road Northcote Auckland New Zealand

www.newhollandpublishers.com

A record of this book is held at the British Library and the National Library of Australia

ISBN 978 1 78009 452 6

Publisher: Alan Whiticker
Designer: Kimberley Pearce
Senior editor: Simona Hill
Proofreader: Melanie Hibbert
Production: Sandy Jones
Printer: Toppan Leefung Printing Ltd (China)
10 9 8 7 6 5 4 3 2 1

Keep up with New Holland Publishers on Facebook http://www.facebook.com/
NewHollandPublishers

CONTENTS

~ Chapter One ~

FROM COUPLEDOM TO COCKTAILS

HOW TO GET OVER THE BREAK-UP BLUES

BREAKING UP

We all know the joys of being in a loving relationship. You hold hands in public, sex is a nightly yum fest, and every now and then he surprises you with chocolate, champagne and swinging from the chandelier. After all, being in a relationship means you have someone who thinks you're number one, holds your hair back when you're sick, provides a warm body to snuggle up to when you've had a hard day at the office, and is prepared to be used as a human pillow when you're tired. Jeez. We all love that warm fuzzy feeling of being settled and safe in our own romantic bubble.

You never thought you would be out on the razz and single in your forties, did you?

I certainly didn't. Just when you were ready to get out the slippers, the cocoa and snuggle up to your man, you find yourself perched at a downtown bar with a cocktail in your hand and wondering what it's all about. It's not as if anyone would set out to end up single in middle age, or that you could ever anticipate how it would feel suddenly finding yourself microwaving for one.

We are quite simply 'accidentally single'. And it can be very daunting. It's a bit like being stored in a deep freeze for a couple of decades and waking up in new-man's-land. For a start, most of your friends are married or with someone to have and to hold, and there you are floundering somewhere between 'I-was-like-this-in-my-twenties' angst and an 'Am-I-too-old-for-all-this?' dilemma.

You're middle-aged for Christ's sake. I mean, just as you've come to terms with your wrinkles and a bottom that looks like porridge in a string bag, you suddenly find yourself spending Friday nights with a TV dinner and a hot water bottle for company. Suddenly the idea of being back on the starting blocks and single at the middle point in your life is like being on a roller coaster that never stops. On the scale of stressful events, divorce or a break up in midlife is up there with the best of them.

Even though the future can look a bit alarming and scary for the newby singleton, for many women divorce or a break-up from a long-term relationship can be the best thing that has happened to them. Instead of looking longingly at your coupled-up friends, you congratulate yourself on having the courage to break free and grab life by the horns. 'Yipeee', you say to yourself, as you feel the rush of excitement, and want to run down the street clutching a decree absolute and a bottle of champers. This can be a time of new beginnings and letting go of the past. No more having to consider 'his' feelings/ways and whims. Even if it's just painting the living room your favourite shade of pink and buying all those fluffy scatter cushions that 'he' hates, being accidentally single can be a blessing in disguise.

Even though a lot of relationships may have started out with love, flowers and fanfare, come middle age, the fun and laughter may have gone flat and all that's left are the daily niggles and three days of washing up. Or even worse; the little niggles that had been growing over the years have now morphed into a daily slanging match, with you flinging your wedding ring at him across the table and him storming off to get drunk with his mates.

Whether you woke up one day and looked at your husband and thought, 'I can't take anymore of this,' then promptly slept with the gardener, or you've barely uttered a word to each other for yonks, when a relationship has reached its sell-by date, there's no point hanging on in there just because you're scared of being alone, or scared that you won't find anyone else. It may seem frightening at first, but getting out can be the best decision you ever made.

Seven top reasons people break up

- He's had an affair.

- You've had an affair.

- You got married too young.

- You don't feel yourself anymore.

- The relationship is more fighting than fun.

- He NEVER acknowledges your feelings and does exactly what he wants.

- He clips his toenails in bed and doesn't even realise how unromantic it is.

Five top break-up myths

- He leaves the wet towel on the bathroom floor. If only that was all, most women would be living in paradise.

- He farts in bed. Again – we really don't care. It either means he's comfortable with you or he has finally started to eat brown rice.

- He takes control of the remote and switches to the football right in the middle of your film – again not even close.

- He's rude to your mum. Come on, he just said what you've been dying to tell her since you were 15.

- He never exercises even though you're out jogging at six in the morning. No probs. That way you always get to be the thinnest!

SO WHY NOW?

It's a fact, that divorce and breaking up in middle age is on the rise. More and more middle-aged women are calling time on their so-so marriages, and realising that the only thing that has been keeping them together is the 50-inch flat screen TV and the dog. After years of nagging my husband, him sulking, me hauling myself out of bed to go antiquing on wet Sunday mornings (for him), him spending more nights out than in, me picking my ego off the floor every time he flirted with a 21-year-old, I finally realised that I couldn't spend the rest of my life with this man and finally had the courage to press the stop button on our relationship, and walk off into the unknown.

Here are some other reasons why women are throwing in the towel in midlife:

- We all live longer nowadays, and the thought of another forty years with a man who prefers to watch footy than talk to you is not an option.

- We have money, careers, our own mind and a down payment on a condo in Florida.

- We are bored of men who don't pay us any attention and realise that we are not passed it yet.

- We can go travelling around the world on our own – the days of needing a chaperone are well and truly over.

- Women can make their own choices.

- We realise for the first time that we won't crumple into a heap of emotional mush just because we don't have a man to change the light bulb.

- We do because we can, so there!

STARTING OVER

Even though more women are ditching the traditional script of marriage for life, that doesn't mean that everyone is quick to embrace this new breed of single sassy sisters. For some, the state of midlife independence is still seen as second rate. I can't count the times people have said in regard to me, 'poor thing, single again,' as if I was suffering from scrofulous disease. The fact remains: dare to be middle aged and traipsing about town without there being a man at home, or without a ring on the finger, and you are going to get a lot of stick! Too old to be out there flirting, yuck. The sheer thought of it. Couldn't make it work, it must be your fault. You're too bossy, too neurotic, I mean, shouldn't you be at home wearing your pinnie and crimson lippy and waiting for him to come home? For a woman who is single and over 40 watch out! Indeed, one of the biggest hurdles to being happy, single and middle aged, is to get over the hang-up of the Middle Aged and Single Myths.

Myth One – Every single woman over 40 is a secret nymphomaniac who is gagging for it!

Picture the scene. A year ago, I was at a rather posh dinner party when the man sitting next to me spent the evening chatting about his property portfolio, and all the while his podgy hand was glued to my upper thigh. Maybe he had done a quick recce: No ring on the left hand, tick. Showing a fair bit of leg and cleavage, ergo desperate, tick, tick. Definitely up for a grope, tick, tick, tick! And with that, he placed his big sweaty paw down the top of my dress and grabbed my breast. I screeched in shock. Did he look sheepish? Did he heck. Instead, he swivelled in his chair, 'Well you're hardly a spring chicken,' he said, his face red and flustered. 'And you're single again, aren't you?' he shouted, as if somehow being without a man I should be gagging for the attentions of a red sweaty neanderthal.

When it comes to being middle aged and single, you are classed as either a dippy Bridget Jones-type character, getting her big pants in a twist and OD-ing on warm Chardonnay, or one of the barmy army; a woman surrounded by cats and the stench of pee, or worse, a wrinkly nympho who is old, desperate and ready to whip off her knickers at the first whiff of a bit of ageing testosterone.

Myth Two – Being in a couple equals happiness

It doesn't matter where you go, the world is designed for two. Whether you are booking into a hotel, eating in a restaurant or taking a trip to the opera, dare to walk in alone and people wait for your man to follow on. After briefly raising an eyebrow, the receptionist, waiter or usherette may ask, 'just for one Madame?' and give you the look, a look that pityingly says, 'poor you, out on your own, must be sad or lonely etc'. We are uncomfortable seeing women eating, travelling and, worse still, knocking back a gin and tonic on their own. It may be the 21st century, we may have sent men to Mars, but somehow we only think women can be happy if they are coupled up. It's an unspoken rule that even if you're unhappy in your relationship, at least you're in one. After all, why would a woman who is past her seduce-by date call time on her relationship? If you are a woman without a man, it's assumed, then you must be mad, neurotic or a bossy harridan who can't keep her man.

Myth Three

This one applies to all those age-orexics who are still waiting to waltz up the aisle and fear that they are going to die alone and be eaten by their cats. It is entirely driven by an assumed inexplicable panic that grips the mid-life spinster as she realises the chances of finding Mr Right are about as likely as winning the national lottery. Of course it's utter rot. Just because you were savvy enough to ditch the man with the BO problem and say no to the guy who put the wedding ring in the chocolate soufflé and then ate it himself, it doesn't mean that you're a romantic saddo with a hairy chin and a house full of cats. So stop thinking that you are going to lead a lonely miserable life and never have sex again! Stop worrying that your vagina will dry up and go crusty and men will cross the street to avoid you.

SO WHAT NOW?

Well, it's time to show the world, that the myth of the gloomy singleton, her head stuck in a romantic novel and crying into her scented hankie, is balderdash! Being single in middle age can be satisfying on so many levels. It can be a liberating time to find your true self, a restful stop gap before you embark on husband/lover number two or simply the way you want to spend the rest of your life. Whatever it is, you are driving the bus and that has got to be exciting.

Getting to a joyful single state doesn't just happen the moment you change the lock on your front door and do the freedom dance. If only life were like the movies, and all you had to do was click your ruby Jimmy Choos and follow the star-studded road to the Emerald City. Moving on from a relationship or marriage is a tough job, and takes time. Indeed, psychologists say it can take anything from a few months to more than a year. Yikes! You could have gone to the moon and back in that time. That's the trouble. Come mid life we are in such a hurry, we don't think we have the time to get over it slowly.

Wrong!

If you want to be a fun, fabulous singleton in her 40s, who's sorted, sassy and swinging from the chandelier in a lurex mini dress and sparkly mules, then you need to make sure you are well and truly over the last relationship. Achieving 'closure' means you have left behind all those toxic emotions. It means you have finally got over being with him, you've punched the pillows, grieved the loss, found a smidge of inner peace and maxed out his credit card! The good news is, with time, effort and a positive attitude, you can achieve inner peace without scratching his new BMW or cutting up his favourite shirts (unless you want to).

GETTING BACK ON TRACK

And this light-hearted manual is just what you need to guide you along the 'single' journey. In each chapter I will give you the tools, ideas and ways to cope with what the single life can throw at you. The funny bits and the not-so-funny bits. You will learn how to appreciate the benefits of your situation and realise that how you feel is entirely normal. So turn the page and lets begin

Here is the step-by-step guide to getting back on track:

Don't panic

In the first days or weeks of breaking up, it's safe to say, you are going to be gripped by a series of mad emotions ranging from blind panic to shock, disbelief and downright devastation. Your stress levels are off the richter scale, and you can't believe this is happening to YOU. You feel wretched and are desperately trying to make sense of it all. It doesn't matter how hard you try to be cool, calm and collected, all you feel like doing is curling up on the sofa with a super-sized bar of chocolate and a box of scented hankies. Aaargh!

So, how do you know if you're in the grip of a post break-up panic?

Here are some of the tell-tale signs:

- One minute you're glad to be alive and the next you're sobbing your eyes out in front of the kindly shop assistant/ bank clerk/ticket inspector.

- One minute you're listening to his favourite song and smiling, the next you're cutting up the expensive shirt he left in the wardrobe.

- One minute you are mooning teary eyed over a pic of your loved one, the next you are frisking semi naked with your boss in his condo around the corner.

- One minute you are blaming him, the next you are tearing your hair out. OMG, what did I do wrong? What is wrong with me? I am horrible, unlovable, I want to die!

- One minute you're telling everyone how you don't care anymore about John/Bill etc, the next you are ranting about how he left you for his nubile secretary.

- One minute you're telling everyone you are over the bastard, the next you are on the bed feeling as if your life is over.

During this stage you may find yourself:

- Mainlining caffeine in the morning and knocking back the martinis at night.

- Averaging a few hours of fitful sleep a night and then walking around like a zombie during the day, banging into mailboxes and shouting at the lamppost.

- Staying in bed until four in the afternoon, reading slushy novels and listening to Val Doonican.

- Moping around the flat/house in a pair of coffee-stained jimjams and never taking them off.

- Crying, moaning and wailing to your friends/mum/relatives on the phone for an average of two hours a day.

- Wondering if you've done the right thing and ringing him up when you are slozzled and sad!

- Accidentally-on-purpose strolling past his office or flat or, worse still, climbing over the fence and peering in his front window!

- Every time you take a glimpse into the future, your stomach turns to jelly and you get an attack of the heebie-jeebies.

- Going around with one of those mega-watt smiles that makes you look as if your face is just about to crack.

- Drinking like a teenager and passing out in night clubs.

Have a romantic detox

After the denial stage of a break-up, when the drinking has died down and you are not flinging caution and your knickers to the wind, you might find yourself entering the slump zone. This is the time where you think: 'What's the point... of getting out of bed? ... of having a shower? ... of putting on clothes? ... of cleaning my teeth? ... of ever falling in love again. After all, I'm over forty. I'm over the hill. Help! I can't cope anymore.

And then, after what seems like an age, you reach for your hundredth chocolate biscuit and crumple into a heap on the bed. Don't worry, you haven't turned into a Glenn Close bunny boiler or become a demented harpy. On the contrary, it is entirely natural to feel confused and devastated at such a big upheaval at this stage of your life. This is the time to work through the emotions and start getting back to your old self:

Just as we sweat out toxins when we run, eliminating toxic emotions is one of the best ways to kick start our improvement programme.

Here is the lowdown:

Take time out: Accepting that you're not going to be your usual bubbly self for a while will help you to kick your heels off and relax. Take a week off work, book into a spa and say goodbye to the world. When we are feeling low, the body wants you to go on stand-by, so that it can do its work and get you better. After going crazy for a while, now is the time to wrap yourself in cotton wool.

Have a good night's sleep: Quality shut-eye is one of the first things that goes when you're in the grip of a crisis. You wake up at the slightest sound and are regularly sat bolt upright at 4 am each morning, your mind tossing and turning and replaying the same images over and over again. Then just as you are dropping off, the alarm rings…Ye gods! If only you could catch some zzzzzzs. That's the trouble, at the time you most need some relaxation and recuperation, your mind and body are a jangle of nerves and anxiety. According to scientists, we sleep better when we feel secure in ourselves and our surroundings, so no surprise then, that home alone and with no warm body next to you, you are going to end up walking around like a zombie on valium.

Here are the best things to do to help you get a good night's sleep:
Get ready to relax: Winding down before you go to bed is crucial if you want to get a good night's sleep. Avoid watching the television, going on the computer, checking emails right before getting ready to sleep. The body and mind needs to slow down so that you can slip easily into the land of nod.

Take a walk: If you are feeling anxious, take a post-dinner walk to get rid of any stress and help you digest your food. We always sleep better if we've done some exercise, so the more movement the better. That doesn't mean jumping up and down like a mad woman. Gentle exercise calms us and de-stresses us, where as flinging your arms around and doing an aerobic workout just before lights out, will increase the heartbeat and wake you up.

Cut the coffee intake after 6 pm: If you are an espresso lover, great. The thing is, caffeine can take five or six hours to leave the body, so having a post prandial cappuccino will pep you up and have you itching to go for a run rather than relax.

If you wake up during the night, whatever you do, don't look at the clock. Knowing that it is three in the morning and you have four hours left until the alarm bell rings, will only give you an added anxiety rush. If you find getting back to sleep difficult, lie back and try to clear your mind.

Have a power nap: If you've had a bad night's sleep, have a 15–20 minute power nap the next day. It will renew some energy and help you to get rid of that groggy feeling.

Keep the bedroom sleep-friendly: Clear away the technology from the bedroom and don't have a telly stuck in the corner. Keep the room cool and ventilated, and if you are a light sleeper invest in blackout blinds. There is nothing worse than being woken by the natural daylight blaring in at the window at five in the morning.

Have a turkey sandwich: Did you know that tryptophan is a sleep-inducing amino acid that is found in milk, turkey and eggs? A turkey sandwich is a great pre-bed supper. If you think snacking on bread and meat is too much just before lights out, opt for a glass of hot milk with honey – another sleep inducer.

Be kind to yourself: Think about what would make you feel better and do it. Whether it's a long bubble bath taken with the glow of scented candlelight and a glass of champagne, or a spa day in the countryside, treat yourself. Take time off work. Buy yourself that new pair of boots you've been longing for, book yourself a weekly massage. Do anything that makes you feel nurtured.

Top ten ways to say I'm being good to myself:

- Book yourself a spa weekend with a girlfriend and steam away the toxins.

- Buy yourself that really expensive dress you've been looking at for ages.

- Be decadent and splurge on that fantastic 50-inch plasma screen. If you can't cuddle up to him, at least you can have... (fill the gap).

- Plan a girlie night in with your girlfriends.

- Buy some glossy magazines, get a bottle of wine and spend an evening at home.

- Go for a long, brisk walk in the countryside and clear your head.

- Buy fresh flowers or scented potpourri to fill your house with fragrance.

- Visit an art gallery and let the art fill your soul.

- Have a long, scented bath and lie in a darkened room.

- Call a good friend and have a mega moan.

Let it all hang out

Whether you want to drive his new car into a lake, stomp on his face in your new stilettos or just grab onto his ankles and never let him go, be aware of how you are feeling. Anger, sadness, regret – these are all normal after a break-up and if you don't get them out, they could fester for years.

Have a look at the following:

Venting your spleen: This works wonders and will help you get rid of any toxic emotions. Besides, who wouldn't fume, fret, or explode into a fit of pique, after the life you've known for so many years has just been pulled from beneath you. Try this: Go out into the woods and have a private hissy fit. Shout at the top of your lungs, cry, wail, hug a tree, then go for a long walk and feel the anger ebbing away.

The crying game: Sometimes all the tree hugging in the world can't stop the waterworks. There you are at work/in the bank/outside the school gates/at home, and someone snaps at you/you break a cup/ stub your toe and you start to cry. Big fat tears run down your cheeks and you can't stop them. Don't worry. You may find it slightly embarrassing, but having a good cry works wonders. The tears have probably been waiting for their moment anyway. And guess what? You feel ten times better for it. And there's a good reason for this. Crying when we feel emotional helps the body release a build-up of stress hormones that could be harmful to the body. It also increases the level of oxytocin in our bodies, the so-called 'cuddle' hormone, because it makes us feel warm and fuzzy. So if you're feeling weepy or choking at the sound of your ex's name, don't hold back, let the tears roll. 'Crying into your beer' aka 'blubbing when under the influence', doesn't count, neither do crocodile tears (aka fake tears).

Watch the weepies: Sometimes one of the best ways to tune in to those painful feelings is to have a full-on blubber fest at the movies. Shedding tears when you are watching a sad film, is one of the best ways to get rid of toxic emotions without having to think about him.

Hankies at the ready for these top movie classics:

- *It's a Wonderful Life*: it may not be about romantic heartbreak, but this heart-warming holiday classic, with James Stewart playing salt-of-the-earth George Bailey who sacrifices his dreams, will have you choking back the tears.

- *Love Story*: Erich Segal's story of sickness and sorrow between two young people in love is enough to get you sobbing uncontrollably. And Ali MacGraw and Ryan O'Neal are so impossibly good looking.

- *An Affair to Remember*: Cary Grant and Deborah Kerr lock hearts and lips in this all-time romantic classic of love lost.

- *Gone With The Wind* – if you love an epic this one will have you choking and chortling in equal measure.

- *Ghost* – all that heartrending… you'd have to have the heart of Cruella De Vil to stay dry-eyed at this one.

- *ET*: ok, so it's aimed at your niece and nephew. So what? Who can resist that finger moment? ET go home… it gets everyone.

- *The Champ*: only someone with a heart of stone could remain unmoved by this story of a boy's love for his wayward father.

- *Kramer vs Kramer*: Meryl Streep and Dustin Hoffman battle it out in this film of career angst and emotional tug-of-war over their young son.

- *Old Yeller*: The story of a stray dog and his bond with an impoverished young boy called Travis. This is a must for all you animal lovers.

Sexual detox

After a break-up we all want to feel that we are still attractive and desirable. That we still have the power to turn heads and make grown men salivate. That said, the last thing you need right now is a quick roll in the hay with the first man that winks in your direction. There is nothing wrong with dressing up and dipping a toe in the man waters, but rebound sex when you are still healing is not a good idea. Not only can it bring up feelings of hurt and pain from your previous relationship, there is the morning-after feeling to deal with. The oh-so excrutiating moment when he is singing the triumphant song in the shower and you are cringing under the bedclothes. Besides, after a break-up or a divorce, there is always the fear that you may cry during or after sex, or worse still, blub in his mouth when you're kissing.

Sometimes all the talking, sleeping and watching reruns of *Old Yeller*, just doesn't work. No matter how hard you try, some ex's manage to keep you in their thrall. Whether it's because they send you the odd text or call you, which draws you back in, or because you replay the relationship 'high points' over in your mind 24/7.

Whatever you do during the detox stage, here are some of things to avoid:

Don't fake it: It's counterproductive behaviour to put on a positive spin. A brittle show of jollity may make you think you are getting over him in the short term. It may even give you the illusion that you're in control, doing the right thing, brave as a gladiator, but it could do more harm than good. You're not a politician and you're not a chat-show host. You don't need to be a 24/7 chirpy character with a rictus smile and the energy of an Olympic athlete. Blocking your true emotions will keep them locked inside you and they will fester and grow. Besides do you really want to go around like a chirpy, smiling mad person with a hollow laugh? So how do you know you're faking it?

You're faking if:

- You're knocking back the Martinis... before work.

- You're already dating rebound man.

- You're staying late at the office and telling yourself you are soooo overworked.

- You're throwing yourself into running a marathon/playing a tennis tournament, anything to fill in those lonely hours in the evening.

- You've already redecorated the house/cleared the attic.

- You've taken to doing the gardening even though you hate nature.

- You tell everyone you're 'hunky dory', but you don't feel it.

- You have watched the entire series of 24 in one sitting.

- You get angry if anyone mentions his name.

- You think you're over him because you are on the go all the time and not even tired. You're running on adrenalin and one day you'll come crashing down.

- You're telling yourself to look on the bright side and then slumping on the sofa.

Don't pig out: Over-eating at times of heartache is a common complaint. The trouble is that while it feels good at the time (who doesn't want to eat an entire family-size block of chocolate?), it's only going to make you feel even more wretched the next morning, especially when you get on the scales and realise that chocolate, not even the dark kind, is not low on calories.

Spread your grief around: Sure your friends/family want to be there for you, but if you bombard your old friend from uni morning till night, you may find she unplugs her phone and pretends she's off to spend a year in a Mongolian yurt!

Don't skimp on the exercise: If you can manage a bracing walk, or even some nightly sit ups during the detox stage, you will feel better for it. Besides, gone are the days when you can go on a sports weekend and come back smiling with bright eyes and perfect pins.

Don't do toxic thinking: As sure as eggs are eggs, your ex will not be agonising over the things you said as you argued your way out of your relationship. He's a man after all, ergo, he has spent his entire life hiding his emotions (from himself). It's more likely that he will be propping up the bar medicating his sorrows away with a bottle of Jack Daniels. So why is it that us women spend all our energy thinking about what we did wrong or where we went wrong? Stop right there. Firstly, it will get you nowhere, and more importantly it's bad for you. Every time a thought gremlin pops into your head, it unleashes a whole army of cortisol 'stress hormones' that go racing around your body making you feel tired, wretched and wrung out like a rag.

Toxic thoughts that can trigger a full on crying/choc-eating binge:

- No one will ever love me again.

- If only I had been less bossy/argumentative/hysterical we would still be together.

- I can't cope with living alone.

- I am over-the-hill and will never have sex again.

- If only I had gone on that diet and lost a few pounds.

- I wouldn't know how to flirt if George Clooney said he fancied me.

- If only I had been nicer to his mum.

- I feel so lonely I want to curl up and sleep forever.

- If only I had said yes when he asked for a threesome with me and my best friend.

BOUNCING BACK

Then one day, after you've spent the last month wrapped in a duvet and drunk barrels of hot chocolate laced with rum, after you've bashed the pillow, thrown darts at a picture of his face, talked non-stop with anyone who'll listed about the relationship 'what ifs', you wake up and for the first time you don't think of him. Congratulations, you're on the first stage of the romantic rewiring.

Suddenly the relationship that ended all seems like a bad dream. You're on your own for a reason. He was a bastard! Gone are the pangs of loneliness when you see one of his socks squished behind the radiator. Gone is the green-eyed monster every time you think of him kissing Janice from accounts.

It's bye-bye heartbreak and hello happiness! So how do you know if you are really on the road to recovery or just having a day off?

You're over him if:

- You don't check your phone every five minutes to see if he has texted/called/emailed.

- You don't think of him as soon as you wake up in the morning.

- You stop saying, 'oh yes, John/Paul thinks'... whenever you're in company.

- You've stopped boring your friends to death with relation-ship talk.

- You don't cry yourself to sleep anymore.

- You've finally de-friended him on Facebook.

- You are starting to find pleasure in life again.

- You feel alone sometimes, but it's not because he's not around.

- You can think of him without spontaneously bursting into uncontrollable sobs.

- You look forward to the next day.

- You smiled at the cute guy on the train and meant it.

- Well done girl, you are ready to move on.

Quiz – how healthy is your self esteem?

When going through a life-changing event, your self esteem can go up and down like a roller coaster. You may think you are about as attractive as Jabba the Hutt, you may think that no one likes you, you may blame yourself for what's happened, or you may think, 'It's his loss, neeext!' So, why not do this quiz and see where you rank on the esteem-o-meter?

1) Your friends want to watch the new blockbuster movie, but you just want to stay cocooned at home. Do you?
a) Keep your thoughts to yourself and tag along anyway.
b) Tell them what you think, but let yourself be dragged along.
C) Tell them you have things to do and you will catch them later.

2) How often do you pamper yourself?
a) Never, you have far too much to do.
b) Sometimes, if you're really tired and feeling like a wet rag.
c) Often. you buy face packs and have a massage once a week.

3) Someone pays you a compliment on your appearance. Do you?
a) Get embarrassed, and tell them you look a wreck.
b) Thank them, but inside you are saying yeah right!
c) Thank them, and return the compliment smiling.

4) If someone lets you down. Do you?
a) Say nothing. You hate confrontation and it was probably your fault any way.
b) Feel upset and get a bit tetchy.
c) Tell them that while you appreciate they may have had difficulty keeping their promise, you don't take kindly to being treated in that way.

5) If you make a mistake. Do you?
a) Mull it over for a few days, then call all your friends and nitpick over

every detail.

b) Worry about it for a bit and then move on to something else.

c) Learn from your mistake and resolve not to do it again.

6) How decisive are you?

a) You are like a floating leaf, what happens happens.

b) A bit unsure. You like to toss the question around with your friends.

c) You way up the pros and cons and make a decision on the spot.

7) You are at a restaurant and the food is late and over-cooked. Do you?

a) Say nothing, you are glad to be out of the house.

b) Complain, but let your friends do all the talking.

c) Call the waiter over and explain calmly that you expect another meal pronto, or at least something knocked off the bill.

If you circled:

Mostly As – you are way down on the esteem-o-meter. Self doubt and feelings of low self worth are holding you back. The next time a tricky situation arises, dig deep, find out what you think and feel, and try acting on it. You will be surprised at how good it feels.

Mostly Bs – while you are aware that you need to make your voice heard, you are suffering a temporary bout of low self confidence. Sometimes we just need to kick-start our engine to get back on top. Remember how you used to be, pre-break-up. Find that girl and bring her with you next time you go out.

Mostly Cs – Congratulations you have a healthy self esteem and sky-high confidence. You're not afraid to voice your opinions or think for yourself, and you have steered clear of angry outbursts when things go wrong. Try to remember that not everyone is like you, and spread the love around.

~ Chapter Two ~

THE STATE OF INDEPENDENCE

HOW TO BE ALONE IN MIDLIFE

MOVING ON UP!

It's Sunday morning. You're snuggled under your favourite cotton du-vet, sipping a frothy cappuccino (you finally bought that new coffee machine he refused to get) and you're reading one of those celebrity mags HE hated. As you flick through the pages and wonder what you should do for the day, instead of feeling the usual pang of 'wish he was here sadness', you feel a strange sense of calm and a flutter of excitement. It's official, you're over him.

You've stopped reliving the relationship in your head and seeing HIM everywhere you go. You've cleared out the sock drawer, rearranged the bookshelves and painted your bedroom a neon shade of yellow. You've dusted yourself down, flirted with the mail man, the library attendant and your dad's best friend. You're back on top. Congratulations!

One of the first things that struck me, when I first became an accidental single, is how different everything is. It's as if you went to sleep and woke up in teenage heaven. Suddenly you have more options than a telephone-automated service. You can choose who to see, where to live, when to get up or whether to stay wrapped in your cashmere blanket till the evening. The fact remains, the state of accidental singledom has a lot going for it.

Here are plenty of things you can do when you're single:

- You can go to bed at anytime of the day or night.

- You can eat crumbly biscuits in bed, while watching reruns of *Sex and the City* and wearing a sticky honey face mask.

- You no longer suffer 'remote rage', aka 'finding that the remote is welded to your partner's hand'.

- You never have to watch a documentary about the war/sub-marines/chimpanzees again. And you don't have to listen to a man in the grip of football mania. Really all that jumping up and down, the gasps, the tension, the manly grunts of victory – you would think it was Armageddon not some sweaty men running up and down a piece of grassy turf.

- You can spread out on the sofa and wear a pink furry blanket without worrying about looking like a telly tubby. And you can wear those fluffy pyjamas with the pictures of reindeer (the ones he hated) and stretch out on the bed like a starfish.

- You will never have to put up with snoring/the duvet war/ him putting the light on in the middle of the night.

- You don't have to put up with the Weekend Wars – he wants to make up a flat pack from Ikea and you want to watch a DVD.

- You can delete the word compromise from your vocabulary.

- You can concentrate on your career, and work as late as you want to.

- You never have to worry about what he wants to eat/ watch/do/or how he feels ever again.

- You will never have to put up with his foul moods again.

- You will never have to put up with his mother/his friends/ his boring relatives.

- You can cook tofu and brown rice without him making THAT face.

- You can do all those slobby things you could never do when he was around.

- You can wax your legs, pluck your chin hairs, wear rollers and a shower cap and walk around the apartment without having to ruin the feminine mystique men are so crazy about.

- You don't have to go to bed on an argument and lose hours of beauty sleep.

- You don't have to clear it with him before you go out with mates/go to the gym or or if you just want to come home late.

- You don't have to pretend the new dress/boots/handbags were a third of the price.

- You don't have to listen to him go on and on about his new boss/his mother/his bad knee.

- You don't have to pick his wet towel/dirty undies/empty beer cans up any more.

- You can spend hours on the phone to your girlie friends, without him giving you the third degree.

- You can watch all the Ameri-soaps/rom-coms or just old films you like.

- You can take off for a yoga break/spa weekend or even a weekend city break at a moment's notice.

- You can rediscover the joys of flirting and kissing random strangers under the mistletoe at Christmas.

- You can lock the door, pour yourself a glass of wine and enjoy an evening of uninterrupted relaxation.

- You can learn to appreciate the sound of silence.

- You can paint your house magnolia and get rid of his horrible black leather man sofa.

- You can hang your bras and knickers over the radiator.

- You don't have to be nice to his friends.

IT'S ALL ABOUT ME

That's the great thing about being single, you don't have to worry about another person anymore. You can hang fairy lights around the bed, dance naked around the kitchen and sing Abba songs at the top of your voice. You don't have to tiptoe around just because he stormed in, in a bad mood. And you never have to clean his hair out of the sink. For the midlife single, this compromise-free existence can sometimes appear as if you have found the golden pot at the end of the rainbow. After decades of putting other people's needs first, suddenly it's all about you.

And what about the relationship trade-offs? Those things we did to get what we wanted. 'If you load the dishwasher, I'll take the trash out.' 'If you come to my mum's birthday, I'll make it worth your while.' 'If I come to the dinner party with your boss, I get to have my programmes for a week.' Invariably one of you would break the agreement and there would be sulking for a week if not a whole month.

Indeed, the unending hours of 'me' time is so tantalising that your married friends, who are still in deadlock for control of the remote, are insanely jealous. While they're trying to get through dinner without an almighty row, you're skipping off to Paris on the Eurostar. It doesn't take a brain surgeon to see the advantages of a relationship-free period in midlife.

For a start you don't have to deal with another person who lives, sleeps and spends most of his time with you. Think about it:

When you were a couple you:

- Came home and told your partner all about your day.

- Phoned if you were going to be late.

- Couldn't just slump on the sofa and sleep for an hour.

- Had to explain why you haven't spoken for the last two hours – even if you're just dog tired, it looks, well, rude.

- Had to make time for his parents/friends/relatives.

- Went shopping for wallpaper/garden furniture/pictures together.

- Had to put up with his brown bean bag from his uni days.

- Had to wake up early because he had set the alarm for 6.30 am.

- Worried what he was doing/thinking if he wasn't concentrating on you.

- Drummed your fingers angrily on the kitchen table, waiting for him to come home/text or ring you when he was late.

- Studied his face to see what mood he was in before you uttered a word.

- Thought about what he wanted most of the time.

- Had to consider where he wanted to live or go on holiday.

- Had sleepless nights worrying about whether he was bored of you, and all because he didn't kiss you goodnight in the right way.

- Had more sleepless nights worried he was bored and bonking the new girl at work.

HOW TO BE MAN-LITE

I'm not advocating a man-free existence for the rest of your life – far from it. But, why not look at this solo period as a welcome break from all the relationship 'stuff' and celebrate what it means to be alone in midlife. Besides, women are better at singlehood than men. We know where the oven is, and we know what to do with a bag of rice and a few carrots.

Men, on the other hand, would rather bash themselves over the head with a golf stick than learn how to cook a chicken casserole. And don't get me started on the dish pile up. I have known so many successful, well-dressed single men who would routinely leave a stack of greasy pots and pans on the side, and only when there was nothing, and I mean nothing, left would they phone up one of their female friends and beg them to come and do the washing up. So, you see, you've won before you've even started.

Six reasons why it's great to be without a man (for a while anyway):

- They are loud and shout a lot.

- They smell more than women and wash less.

- They always want their own way with the DVD.

- They always want you to sleep on the wet patch.

- They always leave the loo seat up!

- They watch far too much sport on the telly.

So whether it's something you decided, or whether it was thrust upon you, it's time to turn the corner and look to the future!

THE ART OF BEING ALONE

One of the first things to get to grips with is the art of being alone. At the outset, life in fancy-free-land can seem a bit daunting. Not surprisingly, after years spent bound to another person, being alone is a very different ball game. When you were two there was always someone to talk to/moan at/eat with or simply lounge around doing nothing with. Then bam!

There you are sitting at the kitchen table, twiddling your thumbs, and wondering if you should tidy up, alphabetise your books or shellac the bathroom cabinet again! For some women who have never lived alone, or at least haven't been single for the last couple of decades, finding oneself blinking into the single sunlight can be a bit of a shock. You are so used to having someone around, that instead of wallowing in the heady euphoria of post break-up freedom, you can soon end up feeling like one of life's losers.

This new-found singledom is different to that which we had when we were younger. Whether it was a single bed in a college dorm, or renting your first flat when you were in your twenties, the state of aloneness meant fun, freedom and frolicking. Life was a round of all-night parties. And waking up with a beer mat stuck to your forehead and barfing in your friend's sink was simply part of the fun. Now that has all changed. A large proportion of your midlife friends are still conjoined. And here you are Normana-no-mates with a pot noodle for one and the entire series of *CSI* as company.

For the rookie single, returning to an empty flat can seem more like a prison sentence than a chance to rest and enjoy your own company. Thoughts such as 'Help, I have no friends, I am unlovable,' can hurtle through your brain at speed. So much so, that we are paralysed with terror and reach for the valium. It's not surprising that you feel this way. Aloneness is given such a bad press that, before you know it, you start to think being alone means being a loser. Well, it doesn't. Remember that you can be lonely among a crowd of people, and even with a group of friends. If you aren't connecting with people, then to be quite honest, you're better off on your own.

So before you start wallowing in a huge hole of self pity, think about it. Now you have the time to do pilates stretches, or light scented candles and luxuriate in a piping-hot bath filled with your favourite bubbles without listening to him shout orders at you from another room. You can invite your friends round when you like, without him grouching and pulling faces. You get to set your own agenda, live life on your terms. What's not to like?

Here are some ways to make the most of being solo:

Get to know yourself: Sometimes when we are part of a couple, we compromise our likes and dislikes to keep the harmony. Now there's just you and the cat, why not find out how you feel and think about things? Try this. Close the doors behind you, switch off the phone and say hello to yourself. Being alone forces you to look inward, which is the first step to getting to know and like yourself. Start living inside your own head. Find out how you feel. After all, without a man showering you with love, self love is the next best thing.

Don't text or call him in a moment of 'was-he-my-last-chance?' anxiety: Chances are he's having lunch with a group of mates and instead of rushing round to see you, he will let you know just how happy he is.

Learn to appreciate the sound of silence: This is not the kind of momentary bliss you experience when everyone else in the house has gone out and you are thankful for a bit of peace and quiet. This is a heaviness that you can cut with a knife. Cripes! You can even hear yourself breathing. Is that me clomping up the stairs stomp, stomp? Aargh! Get a grip! We live in such a noisy world, with so much competing for our attention that a bit of silence would do us all good. Why not use this time as a period of focus and relaxation? Learn to appreciate the unbroken calm you can have when you are alone. Lie back and let random thoughts pass through your mind, breathing slowly in and out. Then, if you are feeling a bit anxious, either go for a walk or watch the news. Getting out of the house to clear your head, or engaging in the events of the day will help you forget the overwhelming feeling that you are alone in the universe.

Don't soldier on regardless: If you really start to get an attack of the post break-up blues, and all you have are vivid images of you and your loved one walking in the park/snuggled in bed, then phone a friend and preferably someone who is also single, so you won't be disturbing dinner preparations or bath time. Plus, she will also know that even if you go on about your ex for the umpteenth time, you will return the favour when she feels a future need to offload.

Do create your very own pamper evening: There is something deliciously self indulgent about creating your own spa/entertainment centre. Mark out your 'home-alone evenings' and prepare yourself a lovely scented bubble bath. Invest in lavish body cream and treat yourself to a home spa. Afterwards, lie on the bed and clear your mind. Let the hubbub of the day slip away and think positive thoughts. Have a picnic ready; sushi, humous, salami and crusty bread are all tasty and no fuss, then pour yourself a large glass of wine, curl up on the sofa and watch a feel-good movie that is sure to warm your heart.

Don't console yourself with a jug of vodka and orange: When it comes to wine-o-clock, a couple of glasses of bubbly are a great pick-me-up and can knock the edge off home-alone-anxiety. But be careful, another sip and you could slip over into sozzled and morose, and end up dialling your ex.

Do throw yourself a 'I'm getting a great new life' party': Whether it's a raucous dance-all-night affair, or a sedate sit down dinner for the girls, why not celebrate the beginning of this new chapter in your life? One of the best ways to get over feeling miserable is to be proactive and positive.

Don't brood for too long: We all want to feel relaxed, attractive and lovable. And life would be great if we could wave a wand and feel happy, confident and in control all of the time. Of course what we want to feel and what we actually feel can sometimes be very different. This is especially true when you are going through a low patch. If you start to get pangs of sadness that simply won't go away, try to change the emotion. Doing something productive, such as tidying the wardrobe, cleaning the flat, or going for a run will stop you thinking about him.

Do invite the girls round: If you are really sociable and miss your old life, then why not turn your flat into Party Central? Make your flat a place where your tired, married friends can flop and drink a wicked Mai Tai cocktail without screaming children and harrumphing husbands. All you need are some nibbles (get them to bring the booze), mood lighting and some music, and you have yourself a girlie gathering to be proud of. Besides all that female support is a great way to boost your mood and self esteem and take you out of yourself and your thoughts.

The midlife stay-at-home survival kit

- If you can't get the girls round, why not make sure you have some remedies at the ready?

- An emergency bottle of wine for those, 'I've got a whole evening to get through,' moments, when only self medication will do.

- A collection of heart warming or funny films and enough box sets to see you through a lonely weekend. I love watching episodes of *Mad Men*, *Desperate Housewives*, *Brothers & Sisters*, and of course all single girls must see *Sex and the City*, for the shoes alone!

- Always have a stash of yummy treats. Whether it's expensive Belgian chocolate, gummy bears or a delicious cup cake, they will keep you on the sweet side.

- Purchase some beautifully packaged bath salts or oils. Sometimes, when we are feeling anxious, having a luxury soak with fragrant aromatherapy oils can help us relax.

- Make up an upbeat CD of great melodies. Sometimes only the sound of a mood-boosting pop song will do.

- Have a stash of celebrity magazines. Nothing beats the home-alone blues more than reading about how fame-hungry celebrities have put on weight/divorced/developed a drug habit.

- Have some comfy loungewear. There is nothing nicer than to slip into a pretty pair of pyjamas or a pair of soft tracksuit bottoms and a fleecy top. You feel warm, snugly and ready to start your evening.

SO WHAT DID YOU DO AT THE WEEKEND?

If there is one thing that the midlife single can gloat about it's her weekend. There is no greater thrill than phoning up a smug married on a Monday morning and listening to her tale of the weekend. First you sympathise as she moans about how she had to deal with the backlog of washing, the supermarket shop at rush hour and the Saturday night TV remote wars. You listen. 'Mmm,' you say in sisterly agreement, 'I know. How boring/exhausting,' you say in the kindly tone of a nurse talking to an elderly patient, and then it's your turn.

That's when you let the harried married into your 48 hours of enjoyable 'me' time. From the morning cappuccino in the local café, the afternoon spinning class/the saunter round the galleries to the leisurely Sunday walk in the park, you let her know just what she is missing. Is it a bit competitive? Absolutely. Is it spiteful? Not really. Because when it comes to being a midlife singleton, you've got to have the edge sometimes.

How to manage your time

Hang on a minute. So, how do you manage to have 48 hours of glam-packed fun? Planning the perfect single weekend is really a case of time management. For a lot of us hard-worked accidental singletons, come Friday night, all we want to do is veg out with a good chick flick and some mind-numbing alcohol.

Beware: too tired to plan for the next two days could mean you end up speaking to the pizza delivery man, the Starbucks' guy and your mum. Not a very edifying trio if you had yearnings to paint the town red. So, even if you've had parties back to back during the week, unless you are a natural recluse, or too exhausted to lift your head off the pillow here are a few tips to manage your time:

Shake a leg! Instead of wandering around the flat aimlessly, making cups of tea and slumping on the sofa, get up and go out. Even a short walk around the block changes your perspective and can make you feel more positive about life.

Have a routine: When you're alone, unless you want to be a hermit, it's important to have some structure to your day. Book a massage at midday, arrange a coffee with a friend. Having things to look forward to will protect you from getting into negative thought patterns. Ditto, going to the gym in the early evening. This will punctuate the time after work and before dinner when you feel like cowering in the corner and covering yourself in a blanket. Knowing there are things to do will stop the paranoid panic us middlies can sometimes get gripped by.

Have a power nap: There's no point painting the town red if you look more bloodshot than fresh faced. The good news is, even if you are feeling whacked, you can still have a good old knees-up. The trick is to have a nap beforehand. Turn off your phone, get some earplugs and have a snooze for an hour. Even if you aren't really asleep, the relaxation will do you a world of good, and you'll emerge looking ten years younger and ready to rave!

Singular pastimes

So now that you have nailed all this being alone stuff, and you can while away the weekend with the best of them, why not use this single time to get motivated? After all, it's not just peaceful evenings and spinning classes that are available to the midlife single. With a bit of effort, you can do all the stuff you like or ever wanted to do, but never got the chance to. Take a course in pottery, learn Italian or climb Kilimanjaro. Following your desires or taking up a new hobby is a great way to build confidence and meet new people.

Here are some things to get the ball rolling:

Draw up a list of all the things you ever wanted to try. Did you always wish you could dance like a professional? Speak a foreign language, or cross the Gobi Desert? Well you're in luck, now you have the time to get started on your pastime programme. That's the thing about being single in your forties. All those things you put on the back burner as you concentrated on your relationship are there for the taking.

Don't put it off until tomorrow: Get online and find new ways to get fit/educated or make new friends. It's fun and doing positive things makes you feel more confident and attractive.

Join a book club
Of all the ways to stave off the lonesome blues, the book club is up there with the best of them. This is a chance to devour a weighty classic or the latest chick lit novel. Spend a couple of minutes chatting about sub plot and genre, and then get stuck into a few glasses of wine and some nibbles. Because, come on, we all know that's the real pull of the book club. We may pretend it's about self improvement, and deconstructing Dickens, but for today's middle-aged woman, the book club is the perfect place for a few hours of female bonding and a midweek break from children and/or husbands, or in this case a TV dinner for one. We can get together, to laugh/moan and commiserate about the state of our marriages, our break-ups and that trollop down the road. Then, a couple of hours later, feeling a bit squiffy, we tootle off home, revitalised and relaxed. All in all, it's a win-win situation for the midlife single who knows she's spent a far more upbeat evening than she would have had watching reruns of Frasier on her new plasma TV.

So before you get stuck into another *Balzac* romance and gen up on the gossip, here are a few book club rules:

- Book clubs are usually quite small gatherings; anything larger than ten people usually ends up as a shouting match. They usually meet once a month and space within the group is often at a premium. Don't be a fair-weather member. Turn up, or else you may find yourself being replaced by a more active member.

- Whatever you do, don't choose a novel for everyone to read that's so long that everyone will arrive exhausted and resent you for having ruining their weekend.

- On the other hand, choosing some half-baked rom com is not going to endear you to the more mentally agile members of the club.

- Set a time and stick to it. Factor in the working women and the single mums to your time plans. Too early and you'll have your busy execs phoning you from their Blackberry. 6.30 pm is probably the best time and means you won't get home too late.

- Don't worry about the evening going overtime. The success of a really good salon is when everyone spills out at midnight a little worse for wear. Of course, the timetable depends on that month's host, so make sure you are not propped up on the table when everyone else is long gone.

- Don't dominate the conversation. Even if you have a major in English literature that doesn't mean everyone wants to hear about your views on narrative tension and cliffhanger endings.

- Don't get so drunk that you knock red wine all over your

host's carpet/break into a soliloquy or simply cry and moan about being single. You will never be invited again!

- Be careful who you talk about. Book clubs tend to be local affairs, and recruit friends of friends. So, just because you know that Mrs Jones is having an affair with some man or other, don't divulge without researching. Inadvertantly dropping a clanger in a room full of women, is the surest way to end up back home alone.

Swish and wish

Clothes-swapping parties are a favourite with lots of women. Get a group of women together and tell them to bring any clothes or bags they no longer want. Make sure all clothes have been cleaned, after all who wants to arrive home with a gorgeous little black dress that has huge smelly BO stains under the arms? Sit in a large circle with your clothes in front of you and each show what you have. The next stage can be a bit of scramble, especially if you are the one with the pair of Manolo Mary Jane's or a Marc Jacob's skirt. Be polite, don't grab. Have fun. If you are hosting the get-together make sure you put on some nibbles and get everyone to contribute to the booze. That way if you don't come away with any loot at least you have had a good evening.

Take an evening class

If there is one thing that will fill in the boyfriend/husband-sized hole in your life, it's learning a new skill. The sheer energy and effort required to master a new language/sport/craft is enough to stop you dwelling on your past. Whether you enrol in an evening class or study for a certificate, exploring new fields of interests is always a great way to give you a much-needed confidence boost. Get a prospectus and see what makes you tick. Have you always wanted to be able to cook to cordon bleu standards? Does the idea of learning how to line dance tickle your fancy? It doesn't matter what you decide, as long as it's something you are a) passionate about and b) something you know you can stick for twelve weeks or more. Shop around. Some evening classes can be a bit pricey. If you are short on money, take a look at some of the cheaper deals and see what is on offer. The internet is always the best place to start researching.

Go rambling

Whether you want to pound your way through city centres, or stroll through fields of barley on a summer's day, going the extra mile with other people is a great way to get fit and find romance. Ok, so there may be the token odd ball jabbering away about bird watching, aka, 'leering at you and making you wish you hadn't worn your nylon leggings', but on the whole schlepping en masse has a lot going for it. Walking is not only one of the best exercises for toning the middlie bottom, it does wonders for you lungs, heart and can give you a youthful glow and all before you can say 'pass the walking stick'. And what better way to get to know new people. Trudging for miles as you chatter and laugh has a distinct buzz about it. And nothing beats the sense of relaxed satisfaction of a long walk. You can eat your heart out without worrying about the calories and go to sleep feeling you have achieved something. Remember to wear the right walking shoes. There's nothing more irritating to a group of hearty walkers, than a straggler hobbling at the back, moaning because of her red hot blisters.

Step to it

Whether you want to learn how to do the Mashed Potato, the Twist or the Cha Cha, gliding and shuffling with a partner is a great way to heat up the night and tone the derrière. And there are oodles of opportunities for romance, just as long as he doesn't stomp on his feet and you don't stab him with your stilettos. Ouch! From rock 'n' roll evenings to more structured time for tango lessons, mastering a new way to move is always fun. And then you can wend your way home, do a few steps in front of the mirror and go to sleep dreaming of a handsome tango partner.

Learn an instrument

Whether you take up your childhood passion of mastering the recorder or you start practising your scales, learning how to play a musical instrument can certainly be music to your ears. Whether you sound like a chicken on heat or you are rocking all over the world, acquiring new skills is always a boost to our self esteem.

Double Dutch

Have you always wanted to master the art of Italian or sound like a sexy and sassy French woman? Then learn how to speak the lingo. Immerse yourself: go to evening classes, buy the tapes, get some French/Italian DVDs with the subtitles and listen hard. Exposing yourself to the language whether you are understanding every word or not, is the quickest and most effective way to learn. After all, that's how babies do it, so why cant you? Oh là là!

Go skydiving

Reach new heights in a jumpsuit and big knapsack, and showcase your thrill-seeking side. Celebrate your single status by jumping out of an aircraft and let yourself feel the freedom. Yes, it's certainly up there on the list of scariest things anyone can do. But imagine the adrenaline rush as you soar through the sky. And then when you land, you are more than likely to want to do it all over again.

Dance to your favourite tracks

Now that he's gone, so has his music. No more head banging in the kitchen to heavy metal, no more loud pop songs blasting out at 8 am in the morning. Now you can play all those girlie ballads, and your favourite rock 'n' roll tracks without him rolling his eyes and turning on the telly.

Here are some songs to get jiggy by:

- *Regret* by Donna Summer

- *You Make Me Feel, Mighty Real* by Sylvester

- *You Sexy Thing* by Hot Chocolate

- *I will Survive* by Gloria Gaynor

- *Single Ladies (Put A Ring On It)* by Beyoncé

- *We Are Family* by Sister Sledge

HOW TO BE SELF SUFFICIENT

Now I'm not suggesting you unplug yourself from modern life, ditch the wifi, make your own clothes and start growing your own root vegetables. After all, you'll only look like the local weirdo and end up with a very bad wardrobe. However, now that you are a single woman responsible for her own destiny, it pays to gen up on the DIY.

Leaking cisterns and plastic ballcocks may sound like the names of '70s punk bands, but when you have one you'll know about it. The bathroom is suddenly flooded and you are at your wits' end stuffing towels against the door. What to do:

Don't pick a plumber at random: Flicking through the telephone directory and dialling the first number you see could have you paying through the nose for a badly done job. Plumbers and other handymen often think women have no idea what they're talking about and when it comes to DIY they're probably right. So, if the problem isn't a real emergency, call your local friends (start off with the male ones) and ask for recommendations.

Do your own DIY: Learning how to put up shelves, paint the skirting boards, and how not to kill yourself with a Black & Decker screwdriver is the singletons answer to household niggles. Doing it yourself will save you money, make your house look nice, and avoid all those nasty handymen who'll rip you off before you can say, is that a stopcock?

Enrol on a training course: If you are one of those women who likes the feeling of being self sufficient, but is a bit scared of changing that first light bulb, get an education. Whether it's how to tile your own bathroom, mend your own leaky sink or how to decorate your new girlie bedroom, going to evening classes and getting some house maintenance skills could be the answer.

Get a man friend who is handy: Of course if, like me, you'd rather stick burning skewers into your eyes than reach for the tool kit, why not have a few handymen of your own? Play your cards right and you can always have a man to lift heavy furniture, put up tricky shelves or do funny things with spark plugs. Offer to make them dinner/host a dinner party for their boss or just say thank you with a bottle of something bubbly.

~ Chapter Three ~

TABLE FOR ONE

THE ART OF STEPPIN' OUT SOLO

GETTING READY

Pink sparkly mini dress, tick! Enough makeup to sink the *Titanic*, tick, tick. Inappropriate high heels, tick, tick, tick! You are dolled up and ready to go. You are playing your favourite song and feeling the good vibrations! You arrive at the party and look around. Everyone is in conversation, laughing and drinking. You smile nervously, grab a glass of wine and gulp it back. Hang on a minute; you can't see anyone you know. You start to panic. You go over to a group and try to engage in conversation. 'Hi,' you say, attempting to barge your way between two unfriendly women. No one turns round. You grab a cocktail sausage, pretend to take a call on your mobile and leave, spilling red wine as you rush out of the door. You are mortified. You slump back home, flop on the sofa and let big fat tears roll down your cheek. Cripes that was tough!

The good news is, it doesn't have to be like that. There are many challenges when you are solo in midlife, and doing things on your own is all part of the single's learning curve. Learning how to be comfortable in your own skin and mastering the techniques of being 'at one' in public places is not as difficult as it looks. The first thing you have to get over is Noah's Ark Syndrome.

Noah's Ark

Well it's true isn't it? The world is a bit like a modern-day Noah's Ark with wifi and squidgy sofas. Wherever you go, whether it's an art gallery, restaurant or a swanky hotel, it's not only the animals who came in two by two, couples are everywhere. Old ones, young ones, happy ones, ones with faces as crotchety as a curmudgeon, it doesn't seem to matter what kind of twosome you are, at least you're not alone!

When we were coupled up, we just took it for granted that we would always have someone to stand by our side as we floated through the art galleries, browsed the book shops and turned up at the fancy dress New Year's Eve bash. Now we are single life is looking a bit different. When I was in the couple zone, I got used to having someone to step out with, put his arm around me when I'd overdone the vodka shots, bring me coffee after a raging hangover and make me feel safe. No surprise then that it came as an awful shock when I found myself standing on my own at a party. There I was hoiking up my bra strap, with no one to talk to but a glass of bubbly and a waiter with wandering hand trouble.

That was my single gal wake up call. The moment I realised that it was now or never! I owed it to myself to get out there come rain or shine, with or without a wing man. Besides, why limit myself to sofa shopping and DVDs, when the adventure is out there. So I pulled up my socks, slathered on the lippy and put together the 'sassy single survival programme'. I knew that even when I was down in the dumps, ready to throw in the towel, or feeling like a wet rag with cellulite, it was all in the mind. It doesn't matter whether you are 25 or 45, with a little effort and a few tweaks, we can all unearth our sassy single self. She is the girl who will eat/party/holiday alone because she knows how to have fun and does what she damn well wants to! So let's get started.

HOW TO UNLEASH YOUR SASSY SINGLE SELF

Imagine the scenario: There you are at a table for one and tucking into a delicious plate of spaghetti carbonara. Just as you look up, you meet someone's gaze. What do you do? Smile back? Think, 'that's a lovely top he/she is wearing?' Do you heck. You think, 'Oh no, what are they looking at? Do I have a big piece of bacon stuck in my teeth? Do they think I am a middle-aged saddo because I haven't got a man opposite me? I know I'm crap. Look at them, all lovey dovey. I hate myself'. You feel the tears welling up inside. You rush to the loo, return red faced and puffy eyed and spend the next few weeks replaying the awful incident in your head.

Why is it that after 50 years of breaking glass ceilings and burning bras, so many women still think it's shameful to rock up to a hotel/party/restaurant clutching nothing more than a Mulberry tote and enough chutzpah for an entire football team? The simple truth is, women still care far too much about what other people think. The old-fashioned notions such as; 'She's on her own so she must be husband hunting', or 'She must be desperate, poor thing', still play around in our head like a nightmarish tune that we can't get rid of. So, maybe it is time to get over those fears once and for all. After all, you owe it to yourself to make changes and open up new avenues in life. There is lots of fun to be had out there. So, why not push through the shame barrier. You'll feel such a buzz of confidence you'll soon be dancing on the tables, even if you have forgotten to wear a bra.

Here are some top tips to get you started.

Stop worrying about the what ifs
We all worry about those little mishaps that occur to most of us at some time or other. The moment you pull off your jumper and realise with a gasp of horror that your T shirt has come off with it, and you're showing more than you bargained for.

What if:

- I snag my tights and have to sit on my own with a big ladder all the way up my leg?

- I trip over in the restaurant/bar and fall flat on my face?

- I speak to the man at the bar and his wife walks in?

- I say something really stupid at the party and everyone hates me?

- I knock my glass of red wine all over the table-for-one?

- I spend the entire evening with spinach in my teeth and there is no one to tell me?

- I walk out of the ladies with loo roll stuck to the bottom of my shoe. Aargh!

- Come on gals, embarrassment is a part of life, it's also a source of comedy, so why not laugh it off and make a joke of it. You never know, it could be the making of you.

After all, what if:

- You knock over the glass of wine and a handsome stranger comes to your rescue and a year later you are walking down the aisle?

- You get your knickers in a twist, laugh and make a new set of friends?

- You bump into a man at a party, he smiles, you smile, he gets you a cocktail, and you find out he's the boss of a firm you want a job at. Life is full of surprises, you just need to open yourself up to them.

Put things into perspective: The truth of the matter is, most people are not interested in you. Like everyone, they are too self-absorbed about their own problems: 'Is their bottom the size of New York?' 'Is their marriage on the rocks', or simply, 'I'm hungry, when is the food coming?' Get over it. Life is too short!

Act confident, feel confident: Even if you are feeling like a piece of mouldy sponge, you don't have to show it. The next time you walk into a restaurant/museum/hotel on your own, stride confidently with your head held high. People will think what you want them to think, and if you show you are sure and in control, they have no reason to think otherwise.

Take the heat off. If you are feeling crap at being on your own, learn the art of making people feel good in your company. We all want to be liked, so If someone looks over at you, why not give them a compliment.

To her: 'That's a great pair of boots where did you get them from?'

To the waiter: 'I really love the style/food of the restaurant.'

Keep your comments light and short. All you're doing is sprinkling your magic and letting people know that you're a nice person.

Smile: Beaming like a Belisha beacon will get you some much-wanted positive feedback. It may seem daft to break into a grin as you read your magazine or look over at the waiter, but not only will it make you feel better, it shows everyone that you're comfortable in your skin and an open, friendly person. People will be more likely to smile back at you, making you feel less alone. On the other hand, if you're hissing into your soup or shooting daggers at the concierge, you might as well ring fence your table in barbed wire.

Here are some quick tips for when you're out and about if you are still feeling nervous:

- Avoid places that are too bright and where you may stick out like a sore thumb.

- If you want to be left alone, always reserve a table in a corner or sit at the end of the bar. That way you get to look at everyone, while pretending to read your book.

- Arm yourself with props. Take a book/magazine to read if you think everyone is looking at you.

- Make sure your phone is fully charged. You may find yourself eagerly texting friends or browsing the internet.

- Have a glass of Dutch Courage. Downing a vodka shot before you get stuck into your meal is a good way to take the edge off being alone. Don't overdo it though, stumbling into the ladies without a buddy for support is not a good move.

- Avoid restaurants with groups of laughing people. It may be easier to get stuck into a gang of merry pranksters and make new friends, but if you're feeling a bit unsure, big noisy gangs could end up making you feel worse.

- Go to a gastro-bar. These restaurant/coffee venues are the 21st century style-eatery par excellence. With their laissez-faire atmosphere and mishmash of comfy sofas and tables, they cater for today's busy lifestyle. You can order a no-fuss meal or spend hours mainlining caffeine and playing on your iPad. Nobody looks, nobody cares, and you get to while away a rainy afternoon distracted by pleasant chatter and bright lights.

LET'S GET THE PARTY STARTED

We all love a good knees-up, a chance to let our hair down, do a spot of karaoke and make new friends. Trouble is, that first moment when you enter a room full of people can be intimidating. Like pack animals, people will often check out the newcomer and give them the 'once up and down'.

How to be the perfect party girl

Feel good about yourself: This is the essence of being a popular party girl. When we feel confident we emit great energy that draws people to us. More often than not our inner good-time girl gets buried under layers of shopping, work and all the other daily hassles that we have to deal with. So much so that we end up frowning rather than flirting.

Think pleasant thoughts about nice people and let that positive feeling flood over your face and into your being. This is not the time to start brooding about your ex, unless you want to look like an angry banshee.

Unleash your inner child: Good party girls are playful and have a sense of fun and adventure. So if you want to bring out your merry side, unleash you inner seven year old. Do something childlike each day. Laugh a lot, play silly games, walk barefoot in the park. See life, not as something you have to deal with, but as a new adventure.

Make a diva entrance: Rocking up in a nude body suit and towering platforms is great if you're Gwen Stefani or any other out-there celebrity, but for the rest of us, making an entrance is more about how you carry yourself. Getting your posture and your expression right is half the battle when it comes to partying solo.

- Just before you set foot in a party or a bar, take a few minutes. Relax the muscles in the face and feel the tension ebbing away from the forehead and eyes.

- Walk tall. Lift your head and look at something at eye level. Pull your shoulders back and stand up straight.

- As you stand in the doorway, pause and look around. Take a tip from the Hollywood greats. Have you noticed how the stars always stop in the doorway before they slowly descend those gilded staircases? While you don't have to go the whole hog and turn yourself into Gilda, (Rita Hayworth's heroine in the eponymous film) by pausing just for a second or two, people will wonder who you are. It will also give you time to scan the room for people you may know and give you time to check out the bar.

- If you can't find anyone you know, pretend to wave to someone at the other end of the room, by the time you have walked half way, you will feel confident enough to stop and introduce yourself to someone.

Welcome with body language: If you find yourself standing like Missy No Mates, you may be sending out 'I'm panicking' signals without even realising it. Before we even open our mouths, we are communicating how we feel. If you are feeling anxious, it may show in your body language. If you want to be popular you need to send out open, friendly signals that say, 'Come here. I'm a party girl. Fun conversation guaranteed!' Sit up straight with a relaxed posture. It shows that you are having a good time and are interested in people. If you are standing, uncross your arms and keep your palms facing upwards and make yourself relax. If you send out friendly signals, then you will get friendly messages back.

How to say hello without saying goodbye: If everyone is huddled around in chattering groups you may just want to call it a day and slink out with your tail between your legs. Don't. Saunter up to the group and when there is a pause in the conversation, introduce yourself. 'Hi, my name is... and join in quickly. The quicker you introduce yourself the better you'll feel, and it will stop you suffering from 'lingering-too-long syndrome'.

Get out the giggle pin: Once you're in, work on the charm. There is nothing more attractive than a woman who is laughing out loud. It lights up her face and acts like a neon sign flashing, 'I'm a woman who is fun to be around' and instantly draws people to you. Go up to the waiter and make a joke, or find someone who looks friendly and tell them a funny story about your journey.

Be a tease: Now you are feeling confident, why not give them a bit of a tease. Teasing shows you have a sense of humour and helps everyone relax. The next time you are in a group, tell a funny/risqué story. It will engage people's attention, and you will soon be the most popular person at the party.

WEDDING BELLS OR IS IT WEDDING HELL?

There's nothing like a wedding to get the midlife singleton all in a tizzy. From the expense of lone gift shopping, the worry of the bridesmaid factor, (you are probably the only single left in her group) and the shame of the singles' table, there are so many pitfalls, you might as well get hopelessly drunk right now and book a weekend away. Hang on a minute! They invited you, so that must count for something. And besides, weddings can be fun, even if you don't have a plus one. There is free grub, a chance to dress up and the potential for romance under a stunning marquee in the countryside. Get out your tiara!

Here is my SOS single girl's survival kit for going to a wedding alone:

The second time rounder wedding: Chances are, the bride and the groom have already said 'I do', cut the cake and done the honeymoon – only to different people. After all, by the time we are in our forties, a lot of people have had the midlife itch, got bored, had an affair or simply fallen out of love. They got the decree absolute, dusted themselves off and here they are ready for round two. This can cause problems for the midlife singleton: jealousy is a big fly in the ointment. After all, they've pipped you to the post. If you are wishing you had found husband/partner number two and all you get is to catch the posy at the end of the wedding, then you are in for some real wound licking. Don't. See this wedding as a chance to meet new friends and even a potential partner. Looking for the silver lining in things can stop you from being a harrumphing single and turn you into being a loving friend who's more fun to be around than a fairground ride!

How to deal with sharing a room: A word from a woman who has spent many nights kept awake by snoring roomies. Don't. When it comes to bunking up with single woman, beware the pitfalls. From the guest who bursts into the room drunk at three in the morning to the woman who cries all night over her recent divorce – investing in peace, quiet and uninterrupted beauty sleep is well worth the extra cost.

In the church: While you may feel nervous walking into the church alone, avoid the following: Don't linger half way down the aisle, look for some friends and then shout 'Cooeeee, save my seat'. Sorry, but it looks desperate and slightly unhinged. Play it cool. Instead, pause at the entrance to the church, mentally check where your friends are and walk purposefully over. Sit down and greet accordingly. As a single woman at the ultimate couple fest you can't afford to have even one chink in your armour.

Being a midlife bridesmaid: Again a thorny issue. First off, apart from Pippa Middleton and other picture perfect celebrities – have you ever seen a bridesmaid that doesn't look like a pink meringue? It stands to reason that if the bride dresses you in voluminous taffeta confections, she is bound to shine by comparison. So, if you are going the 'maids' route, you should check beforehand, and if possible chip in with some advice. Also, bear in mind who the other bridesmaids are. If she has chosen her 19-year-old niece or some other blonde 20-something to walk down the aisle with you, think about the comparison that'll be made. Who in God's name would relish being photographed next to a sylph like 21 year old. It is enough to make you feel like an ageing auntie. You don't want to be rude or childish, so why not tell her a little white lie. Just say you want to give the younger girls a chance at being bridesmaid and thank yourself for having a lucky escape.

How to deal with the meet and greet: This is the pre-dinner 'waft around and mingle' part of the wedding day. Some weddings provide a random folk singer strumming his guitar (which to be quite honest just adds to the white noise) or a harpist dolling out the tunes. Joan Baez wannabes aside, for any midlife singleton, this is the patronising and pitying part of the day. It doesn't matter if you have a top job in finance, a full social life and a villa in Spain, you are still a fly in the romantic ointment. From the faux concerned sighs to the tilted heads, the smug marrieds are out for blood. 'Mmm, you just never picked a stayer,' a friend of mine said at the last wedding I went to, as she grabbed the hand of her husband in a cruel show of smug married one-upmanship. Because, make no mistake, you are being judged for breaking the couple code and challenging the notion of being married forever. So what do you do? Punch her lights out? Snog her pot-bellied husband? Or, just thwack it right back at her? No, you do the following:

'Quite frankly, I haven't got the time for all that,' you say, smiling sweetly, and then you spin on your heels and find someone else to talk to – preferably not the ice sculpture!

The wedding reception

The singles table: why does the bride think that plonking us on the odds and ends table is alright? For some reason single equates pesky leftover guest that has to be dealt with like half-eaten chicken wings. So, while everyone else is engaging in scintillating adult talk, there you are squidged between a spotty 15-year-old and the scrofulous uncle who has his hand clamped on your upper thigh. No wonder you start draining the glasses.

So, what do you do if you find yourself stuck with the kiddies and wishing you could bite off your own arm? Here are some dos and don'ts to survive the wedding reception:

- Don't get drunk and fall asleep through the speeches.
  Ditto knocking over the tea lights or any other bric-a-brac that litters the tables at weddings.

- Do wear your most fabulous dress. You don't want to upstage the bride, what you do want is to show everyone that while you are single you are nowhere near sad. Ditto high heels. This is one occasion where you can really go to town. Sling-back stilettos and pink satin dresses are all appropriate wedding wear.

- Don't fuss about the drunken gropes. If there is one pitfall of being single at a wedding, it's the inevitable bottom grope. Once the word gets out that you are unhitched there'll be no end of drunken husbands/uncles/random dirty old men lining up for a bit of a squeeze. It's harmless. It shows you are still fanciable and it's a wedding, for God's sake.

- Do liven up the dance floor. Again, whilst you don't want to take attention from the bride, it is your job is to let everyone know just how fantastic it is to be single. While the couples are arguing about who pays the babysitter, you can be doing the Macarena with the young bucks and flirting with the band.

- Don't listen to your iPlayer during the speeches. As yet another drunken friend taps his glass and clears his throat, it may be tempting to plug in and zone out, but trust me, everyone will notice.

- Do flirt with the single men. One of the plusses of a wedding is that you never know who you'll meet. Ask the bride or groom beforehand to let you know if there are any eligible bachelors on the guest list and ask for them to be pointed out. Then unleash your inner goddess and hope for the best.

- Do mingle when you're single. Approach different tables and plonk yourself down next to an interesting person. You're on your own and the last thing you want is the old maiden aunt telling you her 'love mistakes' over dessert wine and a piece of wedding cake. Avoid overly chatting/dancing/flirting with attached men. Their wives will never forgive you and the husbands will be looking so far down your dress you will be honour-bound to ask if they need a snorkel.

- Don't get involved in the bouquet scrum, unless you want to get physical with all the other single women (who incidentally are bound to be at least a decade younger) it's not cool on any level. Not only will you be advertising your single status in neon lights, it's the equivalent of screeching 'I want a husband so badly, I'll even do this'.

What to bring to the wedding

You may not have a hunky man to bring to a wedding, but check out these must haves:

- A beautiful floral hankie: If you're going to cry when the bride says 'I do,' invest in a hankie. It looks so much more dignified than blowing your nose on a scraggy piece of tissue.

- A cardigan: When the sun goes down, you may find your-self wishing for something to wrap around your shoulders, apart from a handsome man. Whether it's a shawl or a pretty cardigan it makes sense and will stop you shivering as you speak.

- Flat shoes: Nothing ruins the big day like hobbling around in painful stilettos. Weddings can be long, drawn-out affairs, so if you've spent hours teetering on skyscraper heels, why not change into a pair of pretty flip flops or ballet flats. That way you can dance the night away without ending up in emergency.

- Body spray: After hours cooped up in the church and flapping your arms as you meet and greet, you may find it's time to 'spray and pray'. After all, if you do find yourself in a romantic synch later on, eau de floral will always beat eau de pong.

- Breath mints: Fresh breath is a must for any single woman intent on kissing, flirting or even close-up smooching on the dance floor.

- An iPhone: Apart from pictures of the bride and groom, why not take sneaky shots of any fanciable men. Then if you don't get to talk to them, you can always ask the bride who they are and ask her to match-make.

HOW TO HOLIDAY SOLO AND NOT COME BACK A BASKET CASE

Ticket to ride

Fed up with being the third wheel on holiday or spending two weeks with your family? Why not fly solo? Holidaying on your own may seem like a shock to the system, but there's a lot to be said for it.

Think about it. Back in the coupley days, were holidays all that much fun? Maybe he loved sightseeing and you love the beach. Did you spend half your time biting your tongue as you traipsed around another Byzantine church or dusty ruin? Or did he spend all afternoon sulking on the sun lounger and grunting when you asked him to 'factor you up?' Well, now you can do exactly what you want.

As a lone traveller the world really is your midlife oyster. Fancy having champagne for breakfast, go ahead. Want to lounge around the pool all day? The choice is yours. When it comes to getting away from it all, holidaying solo can turn out to be a pleasure rather than a pain.

The pros:

- No arguing at the airport about who has the tickets and did you pack the passports! Aargh!

- You ALWAYS get the aisle/window seat on the plane.

- You can avoid, 'help I've got nothing to say to him syndrome', as you sit silently at the local Greek taverna wishing you were back home in front of the telly.

- You get to talk to/kiss the handsome waiter who is half your age.

- You can shop till you drop without having to explain yourself.

- You can get up when you want, without having maps waved in your face and being told that 'the tour bus is about to leave!'

- You can spend all day on the beach and drink cocktails with the locals.

- You can have room service every night if you feel like it.

Top five things us singles go on holiday for

A tan: so what if it is not the healthiest thing on the earth. Coming back with a golden glow is a boost to any single girl's self-esteem. Just remember to slather on the factor 30.

Romance: On Planet Single, every moment is a chance to meet 'the one'. Even if we are on a yoga retreat with ten other women, or canoeing down a fast-moving rapid, romance is always in the back of our minds.

Detoxing: For the stressed-out modern single, getting healthy on our hols is up there with the best of them. Gone are the days when we partied till dawn, slept till noon and then lay out in the scorching sun like nubile starfish. Nowadays, it's a quick glass of sangria, put on the eye mask and catch up on the beauty sleep. And, of course, holidays are the perfect time to catch up on our rest and relaxation.

Making new friends: Away from the stresses of everyday life, the relaxed singleteer is far more ready to be friendly. On her own and eager to talk, she thinks nothing of striking up light-hearted banter with the people on the train/boat or even at the local bar. Then back home she has a whole new gang of people to call on in those 'I'm on my own' moments.

A hook up: Tired of the Rampant Rabbit? Haven't had a decent snog in ages? Why not take advantage of some native love and affection. The great thing about the holiday one-night-stand or even a two-week fling, is that there are no repercussions back home. It's your guilty secret and the perfect way to get over the ex, especially if he has found someone new.

The last resort

Of course, you may not want to plunge head-long into a ten-day break with only your Blackberry for company. If you have misgivings about spending your holiday alone, why not start off with a weekend break? With just two days of time alone you can see whether you are a born single traveller or more of a group animal.

The city break: Alone, but surrounded by people and noise, this is the perfect mini holiday for the singleteer. You can spend your days sipping coffee at the pavement cafés or bury yourself in the city's culture and museums. When I spent a week in New York alone, I never once felt lonely. During the day, I traipsed the city streets and chatted to people in bars and cafes. At night, tired and content, I ordered room service and watched American TV. It was one of the best vacations I have ever had.

The country house weekend: Lone travellers are often reluctant to book a weekend break, for the simple reason that they think it's couple-only territory. True: you can't step outside your room without bumping into moony-eyed, hand-holding twosomes, but does that matter? If you can put your couple resentments on the back burner, You may find that a two-night country break is therapeutic. You can have a large breakfast in bed and lounge around till noon. In the afternoon there are long walks or maybe a swim in the hotel pool and a sauna in the spa. And, if you want to avoid the pungent air of romance in the dining room in the evening, opt for room service and a DVD (lots of hotels have piles of DVDs at reception).

The spa weekend: With its fluffy towels, hour-long massages and mango body scrub, the spa break is the single girl's godsend. You get to beautify, pamper and relax in pleasant surroundings, and there is always someone to talk to over dinner. With the emphasis on revitalisation and relaxation, the spa break is the ultimate detox after a nasty break-up.

The group holiday

What happens if you are sick and tired of spending time on your own again? Or, if you would rather be at home and miserable, than vacation solo. Don't worry. For today's lone traveller there are so many 'group' options available, that you never have to say 'table for one' again. These all-in-one holidays, where everything is taken care of, from the moment you pour off the aeroplane to the farewell hug at base camp, are a godsend for the lone traveller who is fed up with drinking alone at the hotel bar.

Here is the lowdown:

The singles' cruise: Sun, sex and the high seas, or just a chance to read, sunbathe and chat to like-minded people, the singles cruise is plain sailing. There is guaranteed company 24/7, and a real chance to make new friends. Everyone is in the same boat (literally) so there is none of the couple/single division. From the welcome party to dance lessons on deck, a lot of singles' cruises are really floating parties. To be sure you know what you are getting check beforehand. Some still ask guests to dress up for dinner and the Captain's table, others will have wet T-shirt competitions.

The holistic holiday: Sharing a yurt and eating breakfast with 50 other singletons is not for the faint-hearted. Painting classes, belly dancing or a bit of soul searching are usually on offer on these organised breaks, as are lots of copping off and group dynamics. If you like living in close quarters with 80 other people in search of emotional enlightenment then this is the place for you.

Girlie yoga retreat: Whether you choose a back-to-nature ashram or a hotel in the middle of nowhere, the yoga retreat is a mixture of heaven and getting up at 5 am! Even if you can choose to stay in bed, you are paying for the yoga, so hey you might as well go to it. It's the perfect place to find your inner guru and go zen. Chill out on your own in the afternoon and have a chinwag around the group table in the evening. All-in-all, if you like your vacation with a few sun salutations and girlie chatter then this one is for you.

To bare or not to bare

Whip off your bikini top on a beach/yacht/holistic holiday? Are you kidding? Stripping down to what is basically a pair of patterned knickers and bra is bad enough, but going topless in public in your forties? Get outta here. And yet, there is a lot to be said for sunbathing half naked. Celebrities are forever discarding their bikini tops in favour of a bit of au natural. Think Kate Moss, Heidi Klum and Elle Macpherson who regularly fling caution and their top halves to the wind. It's the only way you're going to avoid those white triangles and get an all-over tan. And besides, it says 'I am free-spirited and confident about my body.' Of course – like most things that push the envelope – there are rules. Here are some topless tips to consider:

- Avoid swinging breast syndrome: This is when the topless sunbather suddenly thinks it would be a great idea to play a bit of beach tennis, and somehow forgets to cover up. Even if you are of the champagne-glass boob variety, it's never a good look. Jumping up and down, your mammaries jiggling in the wind? Come on!

- Cover up when you go to the beach bar or any place that is not for direct sunbathing. What is insouciant and girlie on the beach or round the swimming pool, just becomes embarrassingly inappropriate anywhere else. Avoid at all costs.

- Avoid parks and riverside public places that are usually jam-packed with young families. The parents will tut and wag their fingers and the under-tens will just laugh and point at you.

- Check in the mirror first: If they really do hang down to your navel, beware the spaniel's ears effect. This becomes especially apparent when lying flat out on the sun-lounger. If in doubt cover up.

- Nipple decoration may have been all the rage at Woodstock in the 1960s, but unless you are a die-hard hippie, leave it alone.

- If you are on a group holiday maybe you should defer to the host. Pulling off your top after an hour's yoga may offend the rest of the group. Or you may just be breaking the sartorial ice and starting a new trend. It's a judgement call!

~ Chapter Four ~

A SQUARE PEG IN A ROUND HOLE

HOW TO DEAL WITH OTHER PEOPLE

WHEN YOU'RE SINGLE

WHAT YOUR FRIENDS THINK OF YOU

Has the phone suddenly stopped ringing? Have the dinner party invites shrivelled up like a dead leaf? While you may be enjoying life in the solo lane – getting out of bed when you feel like it and flitting around town with your single gal pals – some people, and that includes your coupled-up friends, may not react as well to your new liberated status. There may be more midlife singletons than ever before, but trust me, you are still a square peg in a round hole.

For a start:

- Everyone else is making do, compromising and going
  with the flow. You know, checking each other's schedules
  before they make an arrangement for a girls' night out. You
  are living the life of Riley, with your week chock-a-block
  with dates and your new pair of Jimmy Choo mules ready
  to party. Not good if you want to fit in.

- You muck up the supper party arrangements – uneven
  numbers are always a bore for the hostess, and does
  she really want to have to search for a stand-in man just
  for you?

- You rock up in your new leopard-skin leggings and regale
  your couply friends with stories of nightclub goings on
  and other solo escapades. The women are jealous and the
  men want to hear more. Nul points!

- For the men, you are a stark reminder of what life was like
  before they had to ask permission to spend the evening
  with the boys.

- If you do wear a low-cut designer dress, the women will think you are a middle-aged skank, and if you cover up in crimpelene, the men will think you are a middle-aged frump and mistake you for a hat stand.

- They are sitting around the table laughing and joshing about who puts the trash out and how they are desperate to get rid of the Atlas lamp, ha ha, while you are making origami shapes with a napkin and wondering when it'll be a polite time to say, 'Gotta go. Money's run out of the meter'.

That's the trouble with being single in your forties: Most people are either smug marrieds or partnered up. They may well be on the beta-blockers, sleep in separate beds or haven't spoken for a month, but none of that matters because they're still together. And here is the thing. Getting divorced or separating from a partner throws a spanner in the matrimonial works. You cast the seed of doubt over other's own fragile relationships. After all, if it can happen to you, then... So, while your good friends will always stick by you, there are those out there who are not so kind.

Who let the singles out?

The bone of contention is that no matter what you do or how you dress, whether you wear a tent, flat lace-up shoes and cow dung in your hair, if you are single when everyone else has hooked up, to the other women you are a dangerous piranha who may steal their husbands as soon as you clap eyes on them.

In today's dating climate, married women are scared, very, very scared. After all, a good man is like a condo by the sea – rare. So, if they have one, they are sure as hell not going to let you get anywhere near him. It doesn't make a jot of difference that you don't care about their other halves. As far as they're concerned, you are a dangerous, loose cannon, a mad, sad singleton gadding about town, your nostrils flared for the merest whiff of testosterone. 'Lock up yer men,' the women cry, as you stride into the room. Really, you might as well have a neon sign with bells on it proclaiming, 'Single and desperate for any male attention'. It has always puzzled me as to why these wives flatter themselves that, just because you are without a man, you should want to drag their hubbies off for a quick leg over in between the entrée and the main course. If you dare to appear at a gathering where the majority of people are middle aged and married you had better tread carefully.

How to handle clingy wives and sex-starved hubbies

What to do if you get withering glances from the married women. If you want to maintain the status quo, why not put the women at ease. When you go up to a couple, be open and chatty. Make sure you do most of the talking and smiling to her, with an occasional polite glance at him. Whatever you do, don't crack any racy jokes and cackle – that is perceived as strict loose woman behaviour. Keep your body language neutral, no hair flicking, smiling, head tilting – anything that could be misjudged as leading her man on. This may seem like a tall order and it is. But you don't really want to burn bridges. Of course, if this doesn't work and they still give you the evil eye, turn on your heels and speak to someone else.

What to do if the husband comes to talk to you: Be chatty and friendly; it is a social gathering after all. If the wife doesn't trust him, she will make a beeline for you within minutes. She will clamp her arm around him in a vice-like grip, so be sure to read the subtext, which clearly says 'hands off my man'. Take the high road and smile. Ask some open-ended questions that she has to answer; this will either put her at her ease, or incense her so much she will lead her husband away to the ice sculpture. Either way, you have remained calm and collected.

What to do if the husband makes a pass at you: You may think this scenario unlikely if his wife is in the same room. Think again. After a few glasses of port, there are men out there who are hell bent on a bit of girlie groping – and you may be their prime target. Why? Because you're single and in their mind that means no burly protector lurking in the shadows to whack them in the goolies. Plus, the male ego is primed to think that any woman who is single with a pulse is after them. So, beware their sweaty hand on your breast just as you start talking about the state of the countryside. If you find yourself on the receiving end of an unwanted grope, or even if their hand starts to snake its way round your waist, disengage immediately! It may be their fault, but you will be named, blamed and shamed, and crossed unceremoniously off the dinner party list. Make no mistake about it.

What to do if someone does the dance-floor feel-up: This one deserves a separate category, simply because the bear-hug dance or worse the hand clamped firmly on your buttock are common occurrences at drunken weddings and parties. The fact remains that at these gatherings you will often find yourself dancing with random men. What's the harm you think, as some middle-aged bloke grabs you and twirls you around the floor pulling you to him in a clumsy embrace? Should you push him away? It's a wedding after all so isn't it harmless? Just watch out. If his wife or her friend spots you in a forbidden clinch, there will be whispering, pointing and again you will be blamed. The best thing to do is to side step any random lunges and maintain a dance on your own. If you really must partner up on the dance floor, then ask his wife permission first.

What to do if your male colleague wants to sleep with you: As if being single in middle age wasn't hard enough, as soon as your co-workers realise that you are 'on your own', the office lothario will come crawling out of the woodwork and make a beeline for you. With the same amount of energy reserved for hostile takeovers, Mr Office Casanova will do everything in his power to get you into his grasp. From leaning over your desk and letting his eau de creep waft over you to grabbing your behind as you go to the ladies, he will be the office nuisance you never knew existed. Tell him you are not interested in men at the moment, and when you are he will be the last to know.

MIND THE GAP

So there you are sitting in your new home. You are semi-content. You have fairy lights over your bed and a beautiful chaise longue. You are finally making a new life for yourself, and bobbing along nicely. You want to share your new-found freedom with your friends. You pick up the phone, chatter on, only to find there is silence on the end of the line. What was that you think? Well, let me tell you. You have just encountered the married-single divide.

It's a fact of life that what divides midlife friendships more than anything else, and that includes money, is whether you are a couple or not. The truth is, as soon as you de-man yourself, your life and those of your married friends become worlds apart. She wants to drone on about the ongoing snoring situation and how she is getting two hours' sleep a night, and you want to tell her about the cute guy you met at your weekly salsa class. You see; not so similar. As more and more women are single at midlife, the compatibility chasm is getting wider.

They think:

- You are needy and clingy.

- You have turned into a self-centred gad about town.

- You will cop off with the first man with a pulse and that includes their husband.

- You have turned into a teenager, just because every time you see them you are nursing a hangover.

- You are one of life's losers in love.

- Your misery will rub off on them, so they won't invite you round anymore.

We think:

- They are obsessed with their relationship and unavailable for chats.

- They are like our parents. Well we do tend to act more grown up when we are in a proper relationship.

- They are callous for dropping us off their party list.

- Please don't come out clubbing with me, you will only tell me not to drink, then make sure I'm in bed by midnight.

- They should get a makeover and buy some new clothes.

- They should jolly well listen to us moaning on about being lonely.

Don't we?

So what to do? You don't want to lose your entire stack of married friends now do you? And, they should be wary of being judgemental. After all, one day they may find themselves in your boat. The truth is, that when we become single in middle age our lives change and their lives don't. We change in many ways as we cope with new challenges and slowly try to reinvent ourselves. Naturally, our married friends are stuck in their groove. They carry on with the same concerns, thoughts and cosy routines, and are more likely to pick up the phone to a friend who shares their highs and lows. Not only that; sometimes when things aren't rosy on planet married, they may find themselves resenting the sparkly reinvented you. There you are with a brand new hair-do, the latest make-up and interesting social life and there they are still wearing their hair in a bun and with no new clothing purchases for yonks. So, if you find they don't call you, spare a thought. If you find that they really don't want you around or are particularly off hand, then you might as well throw in the towel and hang out with your new single gal pals.

On the other hand, if this is just a learning curve, don't give up just yet. Just because your lives are worlds apart, you are still friends.

Why not:

- Invite them out for a coffee and see how they feel about your new status? It is amazing what hidden resentments are lying just below the surface.

- See what you can do to reassure them? Often people get their lines crossed and think the worst. Show them you haven't changed and that they mean a lot to you as a friend. Chances are, they will feel needed and try and help you.

- Tell her some funny anecdotes of life alone and bring her into your world? Ask for her help or advice? Confide in her about how lonely you feel sometimes? She will probably reach out to help you and invite you round.

Beware the green-eyed monster

It comes as no surprise that some of your friends/acquaintances/work colleagues will be jealous of your single status. These are probably the unhappily married ones, who look at you and wish they had your life. Maybe they have a mean partner and they yearn to up sticks and join the ranks of the lone rangers. Maybe they are trapped with mortgages and young kids. Whatever the reason, some women will resent you for having the guts to quit while still ahead. The point is, these women won't tell you how they envy your new freedom, and they certainly won't be admitting to the fact that they don't want to spend time with their boring husband. Why? Because women aren't always that nice to each other. And hiding in the background of every jealous sister, will be a slither of competitiveness that no matter how bad they feel, they will shore up their self esteem by putting you down.

So how do you know if your work colleague/friend is being downright spiteful? She will:

- Give you one of those looks reserved for elderly patients going ga ga. 'There, there' she will be saying, 'is everything ok?' as she grips your arm in faux sisterly compassion and looks at you as if you've just been diagnosed with a rare disease. Be careful. She doesn't mean a word of it. She's trying to make you feel as if you're a wet rag and she is the happy one. If you are on the receiving end of this attack, simply smile and say, 'life couldn't be better, thank you'.

- Drop the names of couples into the conversation like little bombs, 'Oh, we saw so and so last weekend, there were ten of us all together, it was so great'. Try not to listen to her. If you aren't careful, you may find yourself feeling like Missy No Man and rush off to throw yourself at the feet of the first man you see.

- Pick holes in your appearance. 'Mmm, that's a nice dress. My cleaner has one just like it.' Or she may shake her head and say, 'Wow that's great. Did you borrow it from your daughter?' ergo – you look like mutton dressed as a slapper.

- Give you the 'eyebrow raise' as she looks from you to a colleague and tuts. Don't go there. It means nothing. She wants to make you feel bad.

- Stop talking when you come in the room.

So what do you do when faced with a spot of sisterly sabotage?

Here are some ways to stay cool, calm and collected:

Whatever you do don't get upset: After all, that's the effect she's aiming for. What better way to win the hitched/non-hitched battle than to watch you bluster and fluster. This not only proves to everyone that she has won, but also suggests to everyone that you are an unhinged mad singleton.

You've heard the saying, 'Don't get mad. Get even"? We all have to deal with nasty people. If you find yourself stung by an unfair and untrue comment don't get so flustered that your face goes puce. Cool down and pause for a second to collect yourself. Then do one of the following:

The witty counter attack: If you are one of those rare people who have a stinging comment ready at any moment, use liberally and watch her crumble: 'I have a dress just like yours, only two sizes smaller.'

Disengage: Simply walk away, not only will she get the message, everyone else will too and you haven't had to say anything. Or smile, turn your back on her and talk to someone else.

Agree with her: There is nothing a bitch hates as much as being outsmarted.

HOW TO BE A MIDLIFE BIGHEAD

Sometimes when we are down, we hunch our shoulders and act a bit like Eyore on a bad day. Now it may not be nice, but there are those who just may take advantage of it. So if you want to protect yourself, the best way is to let everyone know just how great you are. Even if you have to fake it!

It's time to embrace your single life and make sure others do too. And that means letting everyone know that being single has got its good points. Ok, so no one likes a braying show-off who makes everyone else feel as if they should doing a hundred press ups and learn Mandarin in their spare time. But if you appear confident and sing your own praises people will be drawn to you. Besides, if you don't, no one else will. Definitely don't apologise for being single.

Here's how to put your best foot forward:

- Speak up for yourself. Next time the hostess plonks you next to the deaf old aunt or the nonagenarian grandad, tell her that you haven't been out for ages and would much rather sit next to an interesting man nearer your own age. If that doesn't work, change the name plates.

- Don't be a shrinking violet. Even if you are feeling shy and scared, if you are at a party, take the plunge and introduce yourself. No one got ahead by waiting for things to happen to them.

- Dress to thrill. The next time you go out, show off your assets. You don't have to look like mutton dressed as a hooker. Simply highlight your good points.

- Put a positive spin on it. Let people know how great it is to be single. Tell them of all the exciting things you are doing. By having confidence in yourself, it will inspire people to have confidence in you and they will respect you.

Brrrr, it's cold in social Siberia

You may find that as soon as you are single, some couples stop inviting you round to dinner. For some, they simply want to be with people in the same boat as themselves. People like to be with others who are like them. It's social reinforcement. After all, if everyone is tired and dealing with daily niggles, and you swan in, in your fake fur coat with a big red hikkie on your neck, guess who is the odd one out?

You would think that at our age people would have got over their issues, found their inner compassionista and invited you anyway. After all, you've known them for ages.

The trouble is, life doesn't always work out like that. Even though you may be welcomed into the inner sanctum one day, when you are a newby single, you find yourself being struck unceremoniously off the dinner party list. Yikes! That hurt. When it happened to me, I was dumbfounded.

'But they're my friends,' I thought. Are you kidding! No sooner had the social sisters found out that I was alone, solo, going to the gym every day, working out the body, ready to re-romance, than they closed ranks, battened down the hatches, and sent me to the equivalent of social Siberia. Brrrrr!

'What have I done,' I wailed inconsolably to my best friend, over teliqua slammers and lots of tears.

'Wakey, wakey,' she said, 'Don't you realise that you've been sent to Coventry? These women don't want you within ten feet of their "I'm probably going to be unfaithful" husbands.'

She was right. The good news is that once I picked my ego up off the floor and dusted myself off, it was the best thing that ever happened. Not only did I realise who my true friends were and still are, I started to give my own dinner parties for the singles who wanted to mingle.

HOW TO GIVE THE PERFECT DINNER PARTY

Dinner parties are often contests in who is the most entertaining/prettiest/wittiest person. The food, to be quite honest, is just a prop. And the singles' dinner parties are no different. Whether it's the women trying to outdo each other on the body image front, a la 'my cleavage is better than yours', type of thing, or whether it's the men vying for 'best story teller of the evening' award, make no mistake, underneath the polite chit chat is a world of gladitorial competition.

If you are going to have a successful evening have a look at these dos and don'ts:

Do *make sure that you invite people who are similar*: While variety always makes for a fun evening, if you invite braying loud mouths with a couple of mild-mannered scientists, you're going to have an uneven match on your hands. Equally, don't invite a solitary plumber if the rest of the men are all city bankers. We all feel more comfortable and reassured around people who are 'like us'.

Don't *allocate spaces at the dinner party*: Hullo, we may be single, but we aren't retarded. It's sufficient to let people know that the usual man/woman seating rule applies and let each person find their own seat.

Do *make sure the table décor isn't too intimidating*: When we give dinner parties, we tend to try to outdo each other. You don't need to be the next Martha Stewart on the preparation front – if you're thinking gold-tinted goblets then you need to pull back. Way back! The best dinner parties are those where everyone is relaxed and having fun.

Don't prepare fussy food: The last thing you want is a group of midlife singletons grappling with snail forks. That, or serving up spinach – who wants to be flirting with the man next to you and find out later that you spent the last three hours with a wodge of green wedged between your front teeth?

Do put the music on: More than likely, people won't know each other. So, when they come in, set the tone by having some up-tempo music in the background. It says this is going to be fun, so relax.

Don't get sniffy if someone gets squiffy: There will also be some guest who goes overboard on the red wine. You can spot them as soon as they come in and make a dash for the drinks table. Try not to worry, this is a singles' party and things should be hotting up anyway. Of course, if they change from merry to maudlin then have a quiet word in their ear. If that doesn't work, find their hat and coat and push them unceremoniously to the door.

Do have 'sharing' food: One way to break the ice is with the kind of dishes you serve. A fondue – which is basically a bowl of melted gruyère cheese and lots of forks – is fun, tasty and gets everyone bonding.

Don't invite more women than men or vice versa: When it comes to singles' events, always have equal numbers otherwise you run the risk of ending up with someone being left out, and it could be you!

Set the dress guidelines beforehand: Let everyone know if you are having a smart casual or formal dinner party. But be careful. It pays to explain what you mean. If it is a no jeans and T-shirt event, then let them know before they put their denim foot in it.

THE SNOB SET

A word about your married sisters. Sure, some of them will be your best buddies and invite you round for family Sunday lunches and be on hand with the TLC, others will take a different view. As you are no longer part of a couple, they will see you as a thorn in their side. So, while you may not care two hoots about what others think, and I certainly don't; it pays to be aware of who your detractors are:

Have a look at these three types:

The smug married (SM)

Could there be a creature more irritating and self-righteous than the 'I'm-so-perfect–and-happy-to-be-married woman'. She is the one who, when she got engaged, did the 'showing off of the ring,' which, of course, was a thundering great big sparkler and everyone was expected to ooh and aah about it for weeks. Ditto the wedding in Tuscany with white doves flown in and festoons of pink flowers. And, if that wasn't enough to set everyone's teeth on edge, now she is married, she is the one who has given up her job while her husband runs around after her. Because, make no mistake about it, for the SM, being the perfect wife is a competitive business and she is number one. She lives on cabbage, does the detox diet and has the figure of a 15-year-old. Her children are dressed in Boden and Gap, and her life is like a photoshoot for Vogue. Sometimes you want to pinch her to see if she's real. She will always make a beeline for you at a party or wedding, and in a loud booming voice ask you how your love life is going. God forbid that you splutter and say nothing, for then she is triumphant. 'Never mind', she will say, putting her head to one side, 'we'll find someone for you'. And before you can say, 'bog off you self-righteous dolt', you are standing there humiliated and surrounded by a gaggle of fellow SMs who have come to revel in your downfall. But don't worry, what underlies all SM's seeming self-satisfaction is really a crippling fear that one day it could all be swiped from under them. So, if you want to stop the SM in her tracks, simply tell her life on the crest of the singles' wave is great, and then throw in a couple of statistics about how divorce is on the up and up.

The needy married (NM)

The NM really believes that you are crying yourself to sleep every night and shuffling through the day in dirty, coffee-stained clothes. After all, how can a woman live without a man, is her philosophy. So, she will pop round laden with lots of comfort food, in the cast-iron belief that a woman can't eat alone and be happy. Sweet and dependent, she needs a man to make her feel whole. Her dating history is a story of overlap romance as she lurches from one man to the next in search of The One. And now that she's found him, she will be jumping through burning hoops to keep him happy. This is why she can't fathom how anyone can be perfectly content with a good DVD, a bottle of wine and an evening all to oneself. If you do spend an evening with NM, make sure her neediness doesn't rub off on you. 'Sure you're ok?' she will say, sighing and shaking her head as if it is your last night on death row. Be kind, reassure her that you are tip-top, and change the subject!

The alpha married (AM)

She is the high-achieving, do-it-all married. A high-flyer with a super job, she manages to juggle hubby, kids, 20-million-dollar takeovers and still win the prize for best cupcakes at the school fête. Bossy, hard as kryptonite and always right, she takes her I–must-win-at-all-costs strategy straight from the boardroom and plonks it on you. If you work with an AM be ready for the 'lectures'. She will be the one who bounds over to you, thinking that she knows best and tells you in no uncertain terms that you need to buck up and get over it. She will then thrust the number of a shrink, her hairdresser and a dating coach into your trembling hands and tell you to get out there and have a makeover. By the time she had critiqued your hair, your dress sense and told you to lose a few pounds, your ego will be trailing on the floor and you will be putty in her hands. Whatever you do, don't let her get to you. It's not that she has anything against you, it's simply that she is a one-woman self-publicising know-it-all, who loves to dispense advice and will not tolerate anyone else's opion. If she is your boss or even a sister-in-law, then pretend to listen and do the opposite. Trust me, you do not want to get caught up in a power struggle with the AM – by the time she has finished bamboozling, manipulating and bossing your around, you will be in need of a two-week holiday in the Carribbean.

A word of advice. Other people are not you. They are not leading your life, but you are. So it doesn't matter what anyone else says. All that matters is what you think. And if you have your own vote of confidence then nothing else matters. Enough said!

~ Chapter Five ~

DAZZLE WITH THE VAGAZZLE

HOW TO LOOK FABULOUS AT FORTY

THE BASICS

It doesn't matter how confident and accomplished you are, how many glass ceilings you have smashed your way through, when it comes to the question of feeling fit and fabulous, a single woman in her forties may find herself with niggling doubts. Thoughts such as, OMG, is that MY bottom or has a layer of cellulite strapped itself onto my back?' can pop into your mind at the cruellest of moments. Such as when you are in mid-conversation with a handsome man, and you are convinced he is gawping at your wrinkles/under-eye bags and is thinking, 'nah'!

Don't worry, even the most self-assured single midlifers are bound to experience existential moments of 'can-I-still-cut-it?' panic. After all, if you've been in cosy coupledom for the last decade or so, suddenly being out on your own will come as a bit of a shock. Most likely the last time you were out on the razzle as a single gal was in your twenties or thirties. You were young, your skin pinged back and you could party till dawn without looking like a wizened old hag.

Things change as we get older. Our bodies, which were chugging along nicely, suddenly go into freefall. As we hit middle age, things that were pert and pretty start to sag and bag before you can say pass me the dumbbells. It's a hard pill to swallow, but the truth is that no matter how hard we try, we will never get back the smooth-skinned beauty of our former years. Back then we could guzzle a double burger and fries and still stay as thin as a pipe cleaner. Then bam! As we hit middle age, we gain two pounds by just looking at a bowl of chips (and you can forget the strawberry milk shake).

That's the bad news. The good news, once you get past the shock of being in your forties and single is that it's never too late to turn the corner and start taking care of yourself. By adopting a regime of health, fitness and inner confidence we can still feel and look great in our forties. If you are having a rough week or two, don't worry. Implementing a pull-yourself-together plan that incorporates exercise and superfoods will help you to get through any bad patches and re-energise, revitalise and help you to look sparkling when you come out the other side. First of all, don't surrender to negative niggles.

Have a look at these common 'slump on the sofa' thoughts, and try to avoid them:

- I'm overweight, no one will love me, so I might as well slump on the sofa and have that milkshake.

- When I was younger, I always knew someone would come along, but not anymore.

- Everyone will think I'm a lonely loser and cross to the other side of the street to avoid me.

- Younger women look so amazing. Who is going to want me?

- I don't have any confidence in how I look.

Think instead:

- As a mature woman, I am more comfortable in my own skin.

- I am so much more interesting than I was back then.

- The men my age are not spring chickens either.

- Life begins at forty... woo hah!

- I have more experience and I'm going to use it.

- Life is an adventure and I'm just beginning mine.

- If I go for a walk/run I will get more energy and get fit.

- I feel great. Pass me the gym membership!

Remember our thoughts are just that, thoughts. If you change the thought, you can change the feeling, and if you change the feeling you can change your behaviour. So if you think, 'hey I'm only fortyish and I feel pretty good', it will help you to start feeling energised, and in the mood to get fit. So much so that before long you have a date diary as long as your arm. So let's get started:

- Think of the positive aspects of getting off the sofa and attending a spinning/yoga/aerobics class. Positive thoughts create positive action and so on.

- Visualise how you will look if you lose those extra few pounds: glowing, fresh-as-a-daisy skin, fitting into your 'skinny jeans' or realising that you have a waistline.

- Focus on the future instead of how you feel at the moment. If you feel sluggish and worn out after a day grafting at the office, stop worrying about how tired you are. Instead, think about how relaxed and healthy you will feel after some exercise. Then put on your leggings and get out of the door!

CHANGE FOR THE BETTER

It isn't just sitting and gawping at the TV that helps pile on the pounds, modern life is slowly turning us all into modern-day slobettes. Years ago we walked everywhere, wrung out clothes with the mangle, fetched the coal, made the fire and washed the dishes by hand. Now we take the car, turn on the washing machine and reach a couple of inches for the remote. The trouble is that our labour-saving devices and modern transport mean our bodies are simply not moving enough.

If you want to lose extra pounds, you don't have to spend hours pumping iron at the gym. With a few tweaks to your daily routine, you can vastly improve your general health and fitness. All it takes is 20–30 minutes a day of interactive excercies, and it will make a big difference to your overall fitness. And the good news is, after a while it will become a habit, so you won't even notice you're doing it.

Here are the top ten tips for toning up and feeling great:

- Get off the bus/tube a couple of stops early and walk the rest of the way to work. If you live near, put on your trainers and schlep all the way.

- Stand up when you are talking on the phone.

- Don't email people in the office. Get up and go and talk to them. After all, that was what used to happen in the olden days!

- Don't take the lift, use the stairs.

- Turn off the dishwasher and wash up by hand. You will save money too!

- When you are watching TV and the adverts come on get up and walk around the room. Have a pair of weights handy and do some arm raises at the same time or run upstairs. By kick starting your metabolism, you will burn calories and use your muscles.

- Don't have lunch at your desk. Get up and move around.

- Better still, go for a walk outside at lunchtime with a colleague.

- Clean the house from top to bottom. All that polishing and hoovering will get the muscles going and burn up the calories.

- Don't take the car if you can help it. Why not walk to the supermarket and take a trolley? Or, if it's too far, park the car further away from the shop to make yourself walk.

- Deadhead the roses or dig up the weeds. All that bending will soon loosen up the joints and get you fitter.

- Fidget. Even small movements use up extra calories.

Bottoms up – how to be fit-tastic and forty-ish

Ok, while integrating exercise into your daily regime is one of the best ways to shave off the extra pounds, if you want to be party fit and looking fabulous, it's time to get into fifth gear. But what if you haven't really bothered to get fit? A lot of people give up proper exercise as they get older. If you have been married and tended to the needs of a husband and children you may have overlooked exercising and fighting the flab. You may have put your fitness on the back burner. Just remember, it's never too late to start over. And there is so much more incentive now you're single. Every occasion becomes a possible hook up, a potential meeting with Mr Right or even an opportunity to get a few compliments. Suddenly you want to get toned, buy a new dress and carouse around town looking your best.

When we look good, we feel good. And when we feel good, we sparkle in more ways than one. So, if you want to look and feel a million dollars, it's time to rise to the challenge and commit yourself to getting fit and fabulous.

If you haven't run around a field since playing hockey at school or think that a dumbbell is an insult, follow our step-by-step guide to getting fit in your forties.

How to get rid of your wobbly bits

If you're standing in your bra and undies in front of the mirror wondering who that woman is with more wobbly bits than a jello shot, don't despair. In their forties most women have some fat that they find hard to shift, whether it's a bit of back splurge, a bobbly bottom or saggy upper arms. Being fit in your forties doesn't mean looking like a celebrity on the red carpet, it simply means making the most of yourself. Adopting a can-do attitude will make you feel more confident and give your self esteem a boost. What more do you need?

Manage middle-aged spread

We've all been there. You're squeezing yourself into your new skinny jeans only to find there is a layer of fat squelching over the top like a big muffin top. OMG! 'Disgusting,' your inner voice screeches in despair. Fear not. If you want to banish a spare tyre, aerobic exercise will get rid of any extra that we tend to store around the middle as we get older. Going jogging, cycling or even dancing around the living room will burn calories and use up excess fat. If you really want to see some definition try stomach crunches or sit-ups. Lie on your back on the floor, with your hands placed lightly on your thighs, legs bent and feet flat on the floor. Breathe in and raise your head and shoulders, sliding your hands down your thighs towards your knees. As you go, slowly exhale and relax. Repeat at least twenty times.

Banish bingo wings

If there is one nail in the 40-something coffin, it has to be that hanging upper arm sag. Come summer, don't you just dread all that upper-arm wobble if you dare to bare your arms in a pretty strapless dress? Girls, if you want the kind of super arms that Michelle Obama and fit celebrities flaunt in their body-conscious dresses, then all it takes is a firm resolve and some focus.

To tone your upperarms, use light weights – cans of baked beans or small bottles of water will do. Holding one in each hand, raise them to your shoulders and up into the air. Lower slowly and repeat ten times. Now to tone those wobbly backs of the arms. You will need to raise your arm above your head (your hand away from your body) and lower and raise the weights to your shoulders. Again repeat ten times.

How to get the legs of a twenty-five-year-old

Now you are single, and the competition is on, we all want to show off our bodies in revealing outfits and sexy dresses. The question is, 'Do you dare to bare?' Duhuh! 'I don't think so', you say as you stare down at what looks like a lumpy bit of orange peel stuck to your upper thigh and pasty white skin gleaming in the sunlight. Well, let me tell you, even sports-mad celebrities suffer from lumps and bumps. Think Cameron Diaz and Pamela Anderson, they have both been papped exposing some degree of leg wobble. And even exercise-mad Madonna has confessed to being insecure about her pins. The trick for good legs is to get a good shape. Walking, jogging or any exercise that uses all the major muscle groups in the legs will help transform spongy thighs into firmer pins. Try skipping for five minutes – it's a great way to burn fat and tone up at the same time.

A bum deal

Is your bottom heading south faster than swallows in winter? Does it look more like a moon with craters than a smooth ripe peach? For most of us, our bottom issues are the bane of our lives. Too flat, too big, more like a squidged piece of dough. Aaargh! Whether you want to live it large like J-Lo or are more of a flatty girl, learn to love your behind. We all have different-shaped derrières, which we can't change. The way to be bootylicious is to make sure the muscles are toned. Lots of exercise, such as running and even walking, will keep the derrière in tip-top condition. Try cycling, it not only tones the gluteal muscles (in your bottom), it will also get the blood pumping, and can be exhilarating and fun. If you don't want any outdoor activity try running up and down the stairs or doing step ups. This means stepping up onto a sturdy stair and back down again. Try to do it really fast for a few minutes if you want an extra quick effect.

STRESS BUSTERS

Wouldn't it be great to get up in the morning without moaning and bashing the snooze button? As we hit our forties and spend our day working, running errands and worrying about the mounting bills, a lot of us find ourselves wrung out and tired. The truth is we are often running on empty.

If you want to get back that zingy good-to-be-alive feeling, that you experienced when you were young, then making basic changes to your diet is key. And the great thing about being single is that you have all the time to get yourself back into peak condition. No more dragging yourself across the country to visit in-laws, no more missing vital beauty sleep as you lie awake till two in the morning when your hubby comes home, and no more cold afternoons watching the Chicago Bears play in their home town. Phew! With a bit of tweaking and effort, you can get back your energy before you can say where are my bifocals?

Where to start:

- If you want to burst with energy, cut down on sugary snacks and refined carbs. Cutting out white bread, white rice and all those not-so-good-for-us snacks that we eat when we're bored will not only stop the energy drain, it will go a long way to giving you a slim and enviable figure. When you eat sugary things or white carbs, the body breaks them down really quickly breaking them straight down into fat, which can be stored by the body and give you that unsightly bulge. They also raise the body's blood sugar level. This will give you a spike of feel-good energy, then half an hour later you'll get a post-carb slump and that's when you get a sugar craving and grab a biscuit to top up your energy levels. Really, too many sugar-rich food literally robs your body of the good calories and will wreak havoc on your energy, immune system and even your skin. By swapping what you eat for complex carbohydrates, greens and protein, you are doing yourself and your body a huge favour.

- Make sure you have lots of protein such as fish or chicken with a small portion of wholegrain slow-release carbs such as brown rice, quinoa and plenty of green vegetables. Not only are grains and greens loaded with nutrients they help give you a sustained level of feel-good energy throughout the day.

- Don't skip meals. Eat three times a day and make sure you avoid snacks in between.

- Cut down salt. It encourages the body to retain excess water giving you an unnaturally bloated stomach and soon drains you of energy as well.

- Stock up on the probiotics. Sometimes the food we eat can harm our digestive system and play havoc with our energy levels. Taking acidophelous tablets or eating probiotic yoghurts will help gut health and get rid of harmful bacteria.

- Drink more water.

- Cut down caffeine. If you can't start the day without your daily cup of coffee (I know I can't, and I don't want to), then make sure you don't have any more later on. While a small about of caffeine is ok, some say it helps to burn fat, knocking back the espressos for a quick energy fix will not only make you look like a mad woman on speed, it will make you more tired in the long run.

- Start the day with a spoonful of manuka honey to give you an energy kick. Then have a hearty breakfast of porridge and some fruit juice and go for a walk.

- Do some simple yoga exercises each morning to kick start a sluggish metabolism and wake you up. Stand with legs apart and raise your arms above your head. Hold for a few seconds and breathe in deeply. Lower your arms to your side and repeat ten times.

Cut down on these toxic foods:

- Fizzy drinks – You may be surprised how much sugar a can of fizzy orange contains. Some brands contain as much as seven teaspoons of the white stuff! You might as well pour a load of sugar down your throat and be done with it.

- Chips or crisps have more fat and salt than a fry-up and will deplete your vitamin and mineral levels.

- Alcohol – Don't we all look forward to wine o'clock? It's that time of the day when we crack open a bottle to relax and unwind. Stick to one or two glasses if you can. This is just enough to take the 'edge off' without flooding the system with too many toxins. Alcohol stresses the immune system and too many glasses will make you feel tired and sluggish the next day.

- Ready meals or takeaways – Not only do they have more calories than a Christmas lunch, they are so full of fat you might as well strap a tyre around your waist.

- Cakes, biscuits or even those yummy croissants wreak havoc on our waistlines and our immune systems and have very few nutrients.

Substitute these body-friendly foods:

- Anything green and leafy: Superfoods such as kale, greens and spinach have more punch-packing nutrients than most other foods. Just add to rice dishes; or eat steamed with a drizzle of olive oil. By incorporating them into your weekly diet you are doing your skin, energy and body a big favour.

- Nuts: These are full of nutrients and B vitamins. Don't overdo them as they are high in calories too.

- Oats: Not only are they packed with nutrients, they provide us with a sustained release of energy. If you can't stomach a bowl full of porridge, nibble some oat cakes topped with cottage cheese and avocado – a super healthy snack.

- Oily fish: A plate of salmon, tuna or mackerel is full of health-boosting omega 3, which lowers heart rate and blood pressure. Low in calories and rich in nutrients these fish are great when eaten with vitamin-rich sweet potatoes.

- Jacket potato without butter: Rich in vitamin C and a great comfort food, a jacket potato is a good choice to help you feel full and stay healthy.

Stress-busting techniques

One thing that can make you feel tired and fed up is stress overload. Of course – unless you're a billionaire's daughter with the looks of a goddess and a bank account to match, most of us have to deal with unavoidable stresses everyday. From crowded subways, lugging heavy shopping and waiting all day for the grumpy delivery man, life is stressful. The trouble is, after a while this kind of low-grade stress can make us tired and angry, not to mention help us pile on the pounds.

When we get angry, have a hissy fit or simply feel tense our bodies become flooded with adrenalin and the stress hormone cortisol. The adrenaline wakes us up and helps us stay sharp, and the cortisol prepares our muscles for action. In effect our bodies create a 'fight-or-flight' reaction. The thing is, though, this stress mechanism was designed for our time as cave dwellers to help us run away from or fight bison/other threats. The modern-day stresses that we have to deal with put our body through the same changes without us actually having to move a muscle. The result is that we end up with harmful hormones in the bloodstream that are never released and end up stored as fat.

Relentless stress is really bad for us on all levels and can leave us with a toxic body and knackered immune system. So it pays to de-stress if you want better energy levels and and a better body.

Here are some quick fix stress busters:
Catch up on the Zzzzzzzzzzzzzzzzs: One of the best ways to feel good to be alive is to have a proper night's sleep. After all, we all know what it feels like after a night of tossing and turning. We're grumpy and weary with the concentration of a two-year old. So how can we make sure we get enough shut eye? Try to go to bed feeling relaxed. Listen to classical music, have a warm milky drink or do some simple relaxing yoga exercises. Turn off your mobile and any computer technology, make sure the lights are dimmed, read a good book and try to switch off from the concerns of the day. Sweet dreams!

Walk back to happiness: Trudging through the green fields, or even a city walk, is one the best ways to get fit, relax and feel happy. It tones up the muscles, detoxes the body and helps you to lose weight. When you walk, the body releases endorphins (happy hormones) creating a natural high. And, if that isn't enough to make you reach for your train-ers, going for a walk turns off the worry button in your head and helps promote relaxed meditative thinking. So, go on, take a hike. All you need is 20 minutes of left foot, right foot and you'll feel like a million dollars. And if you don't like being on your own, get a walking buddy and make it a weekly occasion.

Have a hissy fit: Go on, get it all out. Shout and scream, rant and say all those awful words you wouldn't dream of saying in front of anyone. And why? Because sometimes underneath even the most placid sin-gle midlifer is a well-spring of simmering rage, resentment and anger ready to be unleashed. It is not unnatural to store up feelings of anger – what with being dumped in midlife, or even dumping our other half – we can catch ourselves having murderous thoughts. The truth is, as we hit our middle years, we start to suffer all sorts of rage that we would have laughed at in our twenties – bus/tube/road rage, people -who-walk-slowly rage, pavement rage. Need I go on? If you're feeling as if you're in the middle of a mad moment, find a place where no one will hear you. Go to a park/woods/the front room and start to scream and shout, beat your arms in the air. Or, if you're home alone, bash some cushions and wail and scream. You'll feel great afterwards and just in the mood to reward yourself with a glass of wine.

Laugh out loud: Having a chuckle or a side-splitting guffaw can reduce stress levels and release the feel-good hormones. Watching a funny film or doing something that makes us laugh is also good for our heart, stimulates blood flow and kick-starts our immune system. What better medicine is there?

Read a good book: Let yourself escape into another world. Reading a good book not only stimulates the mind and gets the imagination working, it relaxes the mind and takes our thoughts away from the niggles of day, slowly de-stressing us and making us feel more positive.

MIDLIFE MAINTENANCE

Even if you're in a hurry and rushing out of the door, you never know when you're going to bump into The One. Makes sense, therefore to be date-ready at every moment.

Here is a checklist. Never leave the house…

With three-day hair: Sure there are times when washing and blow drying is simply too much trouble, and really who cares? The trouble is, looking unkempt is fine if you are a harried wife, impossibly young or a supermodel,. Anyone else just looks as if they don't take pride in themselves. And that goes for dirty fingernails too.

Without make-up: A swish of tinted moisturiser and a lick of lip gloss can instantly lift a weary face.

With dirty teeth: Spinach wedged in your molars and yellow ciggie teeth are all fine if you have no self-respect, but a fragrant singleton needs sparkling gnashers at all times.

Wearing a pair of tracky bottoms: Unless they are posh velour, bottom-hugging ones that are part of an outfit, there is nothing that screams daytime telly-watching slut than baggy, scruffy trackys.

Screaming down the phone: I know we all do it. But if you do run into someone you know and you're red-faced and spluttering into your mouthpiece, you will always be a potential unhinged banshee in his mind.

PARTY PREP

Now that you're a re-single there are more and more occasions where you want to rock up looking your best. Getting ready for a party or that important first date is going to require some preparation and effort. This can seem a bit of a bind, what with the lure of those new comfy pyjamas and that box set you've just ordered. Ok, sofa slumber may be a great way to relax, but before you reach for another choccy bis-cuit, why not make the effort and get out? With a bit of tweaking and effort, you can turn yourself into a fabulous show-stopping party girl before you can say 'where are the flannelette jimjams'.

Follow our step-by-step guide to perfect party season sex appeal.

Have a look at these quick fix tricks:

- If you're feeling weary and your eyes are looking a bit dull, a few drops of eye whitener can transform you from weary wench into sparkly queen in no time.

- Prep party skin and brighten your complexion with a good exfoliator. It will slough off dead skin cells and give you an instant glow. Always follow with a good moisturiser to give skin a nourishing burst.

- Apply a layer of light-reflecting foundation to literally lighten your face making you look younger and fresher.

- Give your face a lift by applying a layer of bronzing powder. It will give you an instant summer glow in the depths of winter. Use a large brush to blend it evenly.

- To give the face that 'I've just come from the beach summer shimmer' always use a tinted moisturiser. They are less heavy than foundations and provide an ultra-sheer tint to help blend out any imperfections.

- Applying a mega-moisturiser on nights preceding a party will help target rough, dehydrated skin and give it a nourished, well-cared for feel. Carry a super moisturiser in your handbag and apply it during the day whenever your skin starts to feel dry.

- If you want to rock the bare-legs look, even in winter, always popular with the celebrities, then go for an all-over spray tan. It's not only the quickest way to make you look and feel great, it actually makes you look slimmer.

- Get party eyes. Apply a light-reflecting foundation over the face and make sure you highlight the under-eye area. Brush some blue eye shadow on the upper lids, making sure you sweep it across to the inner eye and up to the crease of the eyelid. Bright Abba eyes using colours such as blue and purple are great for that '70s disco feel.

- If you are planning to dance till dawn or get so drunk you end up crying into your eggnog, then waterproof mascara will make sure you keep you dignity and your face intact. If you hate the mascara goop that can get left in the corner of your eye, then have an eyelash tint. Not only do you wake up wide-eyed, it will last a few weeks and doesn't cost the earth.

- For glossy red kiss-me-now-or-else lips apply a red lipstick and layer it with some sheer gloss. It will make you look chic and sexy at the same time. Complete the scarlet lady look and paint your talons with ruby red nail varnish.

- Going grey and feeling old? Then have your roots re-touched – just enough to get rid of that ageing grey, then add some blonde or golden softening touches for the perfect party pick-me-up.

Party dressing

- You don't need to wear head-to-toe sequins to sparkle at a party. The key to looking fabulous is looking like a sparkly you. Start by making sure you select a party dress that flatters your shape and colouring. If the day is looming and you still haven't found your cocktail favourite, then find a little black dress – a dark colour is particularly chic and slimming as well.

- If you are one of those women who tends to have work-and-play parties, why not invest in a few classic items that you can mix and match without too much thought?

A great pair of black cigarette pants that can be worn during the day and given instant office party glam with a pair of stilettos and a skimpy top is perfect. A classic black jacket will always be useful whatever the weather, and can smarten up a day dress. Ditto a wide belt can transform a plain tube dress into a glamorous outfit.

- Give thanks for spanx. Control underwear, aka big pants, is the party girl's must-have. It can smooth out lumps and bumps before you can say, 'pass the knicker elastic', and help create a smooth sleek figure.

- Invest in a pair of killer heels and give any party outfit a shot of va va voom. A comfortable pair of stilettos (not so high you need a friend to cling onto) will instantly elongate your leg, slim your ankles and give you a wiggle that Marilyn Monroe would be proud of.

- So come on, don't stay in, go out! You know you look great!

RETOX: GOING OUT ON THE RAZ AND THEN DETOXING

One of the great things about being a re-single is that you get to live like a 25-year-old again. Instead of staying in and watching re-runs of *Frasier* and *The Good Wife*, you can breakdance to Michael Jackson, down the tequila shots with your fellow single gal pals and kiss the handsome hunk in the corner.

There is, however, one downside to all this midlife partying – the morning after. Once upon a time we could dance on tables, get bladdered and still jump out of bed the next day, fresh faced and dewy-skinned. Twenty years later our poor middlie bodies and minds are simply not up to pulling an all-nighter. If you dare to stay out beyond midnight and have more than a couple of white wine spritzers you are bound to wake up with a face like grey dough and eyes like puffy, wrinkly cushions. And don't get me started on the headache/sick as a dog feeling. Pass me the asprin.

Ok, so there is no cure to the midlife hangover, but there are ways of morphing from fuzzy headed and death-warmed-up to feeling semi-functional and energetic by lunchtime.

Here are some ways to get you started:

- Drink lots of water before you go out. Stock up on the H20 and you will be giving your body a head start in the headache department. Alcohol dehydrates the body, so if you drink lots of water before, during and after the party, you are saving your skin and your soul!

- Don't mix your drinks: If you want to get all lovely and squiffy and do silly things, fine. But mix your drinks and you could be chundering rather than chatting. Sticking to either wine, beer or spirits means you can drink more without ending up feeling like you've just injested a lorry load of poisonous toxins.

- Stay in bed. Don't jump out of bed at 7 am, feeling guilt ridden and willing to run ten miles around the park. Relaxing the body for as long as possible will give your head and body the rest it needs. Keep some water by your bedside and sip regularly.

- When you feel human again, jump up, have a cup of coffee and go for a run/brisk walk. The coffee will kick start your mind, fresh air will wake you up and clear your head, and the exercise will sweat out the toxins.

- Don't attempt breakfast until you can face the thought of food without wanting to upend the contents of your stomach. Even then, gently does it. Eat some cereal topped with a banana or have a boiled egg and toast. A fry-up may seem like the best idea, but all that fat is the worst thing for an alcohol-sensitive stomach.

- Stock some hangover cures in the cupboard: Drinking a probiotic yoghurt will do wonders to help all that stomach-churning sickness. Ditto a can of cold sugar-laden coca cola.

- If all else fails, have a hair of the dog and down a bloody Mary before you can say, 'Oy stay off the booze'.

~ Chapter Six ~

THE BUDDY FILES

HOW TO MAKE FRIENDS WHEN YOU'RE SINGLE

DIVVYING UP THE ASSETS

It's a fact of life that when you're divvying up the assets after a break-up, the who-gets-what issue doesn't just end with the house, your favourite sofa and the Beatles CDs. Like every other asset, friends will be split, too. This means that you may lose some of the people you got hopelessly drunk with, shed buckets of tears with and have generally grown accustomed to over the years.

When you were a couple, you probably amassed a motley group of mates. Other couples you went to dinner with, teamed up with for the pub quiz night or had a good old chortle with when they showed up wearing matching tattoos! Then one day, before the ink has dried on the decree absolute or you say goodbye to a long-term partner, not only do you find yourself in the midst of the break-up blues, your friendship network has also split in half.

For a start, no matter how nice, warm and funny you think you are, there will be some mates who will be running over to his camp. I remember when I dumped the fiancée who had strung me along for years, not only did he tell everyone I was a whinging harpy, he went on a charm offensive and managed to pilfer some of our best friends, including the entire female population of our local social club! Cripes! I don't know about you, but sometimes the break-up with mutual friends can be more traumatic than calling time on a relationship that has passed its fun-by date. So, as you sit at home twiddling your thumbs and waiting for the phone to ring, you may wonder where you're going to find some regular friends to hang out and do some fun stuff with. Because, lets face it, making new friends in your forties can be a daunting, if not scary, prospect. In your twenties, gathering new mates at bars and parties was all part of growing up. Then, you settled down and shifted your frenergy (friend energy) over to your beloved. Gone were those girlie one-hour phone-athons and in came the snuggle-on-the-sofa-box-set evenings. Gone were the girlie coffees and instead you relied on the easy chit chat and intimacy of one person to fill your companionship quota.

Really, trying to up your bud quota in midlife may seem like climbing a mountain in flip flops – impossible. We feel vulnerable enough as a newby singleton. Forget it, you think as you slump on the sofa, I'd rather paint my bedroom black than trawl the streets for new buddies. Not so fast! Loading the mate-o-meter back to plenty can be a lot of fun and gives you the chance to get out of your break-up slump. During your single phase, you will be surprised how great it feels to be free to make new contacts and have exciting times. All it takes is some good old-fashioned planning, a dash of resolve and being open to new experiences. While making new friends may seem hard at the outset, the good news is that the more friends you have, the easier it is to make new ones. So let's get started!

THE BASICS

How to friend date

We all know how great it is to be with a friend who has the same taste in fashion/laughs at the same jokes and has the same four films on their top movie list, but there are times when it pays to widen your social circle. While chemistry is certainly a factor in creating a potential soul mate, when you are out to carve a new social niche for yourself, the first step is the scatter gun approach – aka making friends with everyone who isn't a mass murderer. I'm not suggesting you use people as if you're a networking slime ball in the manner of 'please introduce me to your friend with all the connections and then I'll drop you like a lead balloon'. Friend dating is based on the idea that we can turn strangers into friends.

Every time you take a trip to the park, go on your travels, attend a work conference or sip a mocha latte at your local café there is a chance to flash a mega-watt smile and friend up. Just opening up your life will add variety and increase your levels of happiness.

So why not:

- Talk to a person in a check-out queue?

- Strike up a debate at the bus stop?

- Comment on a painting as you browse a gallery?

- Chat to the barista at your local Caffè Nero?

- Talk academia with a stranger at a book shop?

- Say, 'hi' to people you've seen once or twice?

You're in your local café and you spot someone you've seen a few times before who looks like your type of person. What do you do? Do you carry on sipping your coffee, head down, without saying a word or do you think, 'why not' and smile? Studies show that people who have a friendly, relaxed attitude to life are happier than those who obsess about every detail and outcome. So why not just think 'what the hell' and beam up?

Here's the lowdown
Be a human welcome mat: If you find yourself standing around looking glum, eyes planted firmly on the ground and arms crossed around the chest like a straightjacket, you're more than likely sending out keep away signals without even realising it. If you want to make friends, you need to fake it. Make yourself relax by breathing deeply and thinking nice thoughts. Plant a faint smile on your face and don't avoid people's glances. Keep your head up, smile and make eye contact. People respond to others who look confident.

Avoid:

- Standing with legs apart and hands on hips. You are not Calamity Jane ready for a shoot out!

- Clenching your fists. You are not Cassius Clay ready for a punch up!

- Standing so close to someone you can smell their after-shave/perfume.

- Chewing gum like a hoodlum. You are not in lock up!

- Wringing your hands. You'll look as if you are going into meltdown.

- Wearing scruffy/stained clothes – it may be laundry day but you'll look like a hobo.

- Talking loudly on your phone, so no one can hear them-selves think.

- Pursing your lips as if you've just sucked a lemon!

- Hunching your back and rounding your shoulders. You are not back at school.

- Nodding your head from side to side and staring. While you want to show you like them, if you over do it you'll risk looking like Tigger on heat or a five-year-old.

TALK TO ME!

Once you've avoided the body language no nos, the next step is to get the verbal chit chat going. Getting on with people doesn't mean you have to blab non stop. Neither does it mean you have to be the life and soul of the party, wear a red nose or be a joke-aholic. The recipe for being a popular person and having a rollerdex full of contacts is all about learning how to communicate with confidence and making the first move.

How not to be boring

Zzzzzzzzzzzzzzzzzzzzzzz has she finished yet? Oh dear. There's nothing worse than being mistaken for the dinner-party/school-gate bore. It can happen to anyone. When we get older, we can find ourselves a bit rusty and out of practice with the social conflab. Try not to talk for America. Small talk is all about sprinkling the conversation with light-hearted chit chat that is friendly and not too risqué. It's a teaser before you get into the real thing.

If you're stuck for things to say, here are some conversation openers so you never need to get tongue-tied.

- Talk about your surroundings: This is a great bar/book store/gallery. I love the paintings, these books on Spain, this cocktail...

- Find things in common: If you see someone with a book in front of them, ask what they are reading and maybe find something to say about it. Say you love that author and ask who their favourite writer is?

- Compliment them: Pick out one thing about them that you genuinely like. 'That's a lovely dress/scarf/shoes.' Where did you get it?

- Open the conversation up: Why not bring in the table/ person next to you and get a threeway chat going?

- Throw in some fun facts. Find out the news of the day or get some interesting facts from the internet. It will make you seem interesting and topical, and is a great icebreaker.

Whatever you do, don't:

- Corner a person in a conversation about the housing shortage in Uzbekistan or any other passion project you have.

- Rant, get angry or show any emotion that will make your co-conversationalist want to run for cover. Besides, It shows you have little control over your feelings and behaviour.

- Sound like a whirling dervish. No one wants to be chatting to a demented nut case.

- Say negative things. No one wants to be stuck talking to the misery monster.

- Ask them to be your Facebook friend. Again, it's too soon.

- Go on and on. If the conversation has come to a natural conclusion, or if they are already giving you the silent treatment, it's time to make your excuses and leg it.

- Rush and gush: This is when you splurge out your 'life story' to someone you've met once! Opening up too soon sends a signal that you are needy, desperate and a potential friendship bunny boiler. The idea is to build rapport

slowly, by drip-feeding facts and feelings about yourself
and waiting for them to do the same.

It's time to up the ante
As you see your new contacts a few times, you can start to build rapport.

Remember their name: Make them feel special by keeping in mind their
name or details about their lives. Not only will they feel important, they
will probably open up and reveal some information about their lives.

Suggest a meet: As long as you have tip-toed through the friendship
maze and neither of you have peaked too soon (aka getting soooo
intense that one of you has run for the hills), why not suggest meeting
up? No one wants to get rejected, so drop it casually into the conversation. If you are talking about a subject you both find interesting
suggest continuing the conversation over a cuppa later in the week. If
they seem enthusiastic, look out for eyes lighting up and a quick 'yeah
sure' reply – then fix a day and time that suits both of you. Beware:
if they hesitate and look as if they would rather be chopping logs in
outer Siberia than standing with you, wrap up the conversation and
make your exit.

Win some, lose some: It stands to reason that not all your friend dates
will morph into lifelong friendships. While they don't need to be soul
mate material, sometimes people are just too different. If you both
babble on excitedly about the same things, and find you have more
common interests than a pair of Siamese twins then take it to the next
level. On the other hand, if there are more pauses than a badly done
speech and you find yourself twiddling your hair and wondering why
time has stood still, cull and leave.

The buddy brigade
Now you are flying solo, your friends are going to mean the world to

you. They will prop you up when you're feeling blue. They'll come round with the emergency Chardonnay, Kleenex and tubs of ice cream when you have a 'wish I was still with him' attack, and will comfort you with just the right kind words to make you feel good again.

In order to keep the single life afloat we all need more than one trusted buddy. According to psychologists every midlife single woman needs five friends to cope with what modern life has to throw at her. Here's the lowdown:

The single gal pal

- You can always count on your co-singleteer to understand just how you feel at any given moment. Chances are they empathise.

- Unburdened after looking after her man, she will have oodles of time to pop round for a moan-and-groan session and bring round the game of Connect Four.

- You don't have to pretend everything is ok.

- She won't judge you or get tired of your whingeing. She'll just be thankful there's someone in the same boat as her.

- She'll be happy to be your designated sharking sister and will think nothing of coming out on the pull.

The playmate

- Armed with an address book the size of the bible and on the guest list of every party in town, she is your golden ticket into glamour land.

- You don't know her well, which means you can't offload your ex files onto her. This is good, as it makes you forget your troubles as you down another Cosmopolitan cocktail.

- She is the perfect running or gym partner. Superficial and fun, she is great if you want some emotional down time.

- She is great as a temporary wingman. You can hook up for coffee and hope to meet more people.

- Bubbly and vivacious she is a lot of fun to be around. But beware, playmates are not good on the sympathy front. If you are feeling teary or a bit down don't bank on her to be on hand with wise words and comfort. She is more likely to get very uncomfortable, make her excuses and leave.

- Save her for the good times. Hang out while it lasts and don't waste any tears when it's over.

The best friend

- You've probably known her since kindergarten, and got up to alsorts of mischief together. She was the one holding your hair back when you were sick, your best bridesmaid at your wedding and now she is on hand with the tubs of Häagen Dazs. Your lives may have taken very different paths but you know she is always there for you.

- It doesn't matter if you don't see/phone each other for weeks or even months, you always just pick up where you left off.

- She is the one who'll tell you to 'get a grip', and get on with it. After all, she's known you long enough that she doesn't have to mince her words. She knows you so well, you can always be yourself with her.

The unhappily married friend

- If you want a shot of schadenfreude, she is a constant reminder that life is not always happy in smug married land.

- Desperate to escape her tedious husband and noisy children, she will rush around with a pot roast, expensive wine and give you all the attention you need.

- She is a good sounding board. She will come round to listen to your stories of parties, new hook ups and devour all the juicy gossip you have laid your hands on as a newby singleton.

- She will provide you with a ready-made family in those 'I can't stand the single life' moments.

The walker

- As your non-romantic wingman, the walker means you can rock up to any event and never feel out of place. There will always be times when you are invited to a party/gallery opening and you simply can't face pitching up solo.

- You can wear your sparkliest, tightest, shortest dress and know that a) he wont be performing the taxi lunge on you at the end of the night and b) he will fend off any nasty mutton murmurs.

- No one will think you are a sad singleton, especially if you fake kiss him half way through the party.

- Make sure you vet him. You don't want to turn up with a man whose conversational range covers property and celebrities with big boobs!

- If he is famous you may even get your picture in the paper as the mystery guest.

The five secrets of midlife friendship

No matter how many friends you have, it's always a good idea to have a friendship tune-up every now and then.

Have a look at these five rules of good matesmanship

Don't be competitive: Being competitive may help you succeed in the workplace, but it can destroy an otherwise fulfilling friendship. Friendship is not about winning or losing, it is about dishing out the love. Turn off your competitive button and enjoy people for who they are and you'll start to have more fun.

Be more forgiving: One of the great secrets of friendship is the ability to forgive. If someone upsets you and you hold a grudge for ever you'll just be storing up resentments and hostile feelings. Try letting small upsets go. This doesn't mean being a doormat. If somebody seriously hurts you, let them know you don't accept that kind of behaviour. But don't take it personally. It's their problem, not yours.

Gold-star listening: Next time you're chatting to a friend or colleague, look out for 'iceberg' statements. This is a statement where 90 per cent of the information is lurking beneath the surface. If someone says, 'Guess what happened to me?', they're letting you know that they want to talk about something. Be a friend and ask them what's occuring. You'll be doing them a favour and they'll appreciate your interest.

Don't hide things: Friendships become deeper when both parties share things about themselves. Telling someone how embarrassed you felt when you had to give a presentation/go on a first date, not only makes you seem human and endearing, it means you are showing trust in the other person. Chances are they will let a bit of their façade drop and tell you their last toe-curling moment. If they keep schtum and you are doing all the revealing, pull back and see if they respond. People who can't give of themselves are bound to have intimacy issues and are unlikely to make good close friends.

Accept yourself: You can't accept others unless you accept yourself, warts and all. If you are tough on others who make mistakes, it shows you are unable to forgive your own weaknesses. Treating people kindly shows you know how to be compassionate with yourself. Think of something good about yourself every day then put that characteristic into action. For example, if you are a kind person, do something well-meaning for others and watch how your mood improves.

Learn to empathise: Empathy is the ability to sense what others are feeling even though you are not in their situation. This is the life blood of getting close to people. The next time you are with a friend, and they tell you how they feel, don't just wait until it's your time to talk, stop and think. Try to put yourself in their shoes. That way you can give good sympathetic advice that they'll appreciate.

How to tell if she is a frenemy

These are women who look like friends, sound like friends but, believe me, the last thing they have is your best interests at heart. Here are the ways to tell if your mate is more foe than friend:

- She's controlling and possessive.

- She is a liar.

- She borrows your clothes and never gives them back.

- You listen to her for hours talking about her mum, her stalking ex and her broken dishwasher. No sooner do you begin to tell her your news, she either pretends her mobile is breaking up or she has to rush off.

- She stole your husband.

- She carries on talking even if you are bent double and crying your eyes out!

- She ditches you as soon as she meets someone more interesting, and then calls you up as if nothing has happened.

- You find yourself searching for things to say when you are out sharing a coffee.

- You would rather eat ten-inch nails than spend an evening with her.

- She hangs out with your ex.

- She always waits for you to call/text or skype her and then pretends she is busy.

- She makes little catty remarks when you are least expecting it.

- She flies into a rage if you are ten minutes late.

Don't be an over-giver

We pour all our love into our friends when we are single. Can you blame us? After all, it's not as if we have someone to chat to when we get home or a shoulder to cry on when the boss has been shouting at us all day. But, no matter how big your love-shaped hole is, beware of falling into the over-giving trap. If you want to hold onto your mates, tune down the 'generosity' button.

As a midlife singleton without children, I am guilty of fussing around my friends like a lingering waiter. I make them coffee, plump up their cushions, get their favourite DVDs and make sure they are comfortable and cosy ALL OF THE TIME! Not surprisingly, I am pouring all my nurturing supplies into my friends. This is fine at first, but after a while they may feel a bit overwhelmed and back off. If like me, you tend to suffer from nurture overload, give your friends a break and go for a jog round the park.

How not to be needy

A word on neediness. A different story to the over-giver, but just as bad when it comes to keeping friends. You don't have to go around whistling and pretending you are soooo happy you could break into a jig. On the other hand, no one wants to be around a clingy Cathy. There is nothing wrong in wanting to be loved, but sometimes when we are feeling bone-crushingly lonely or insecure we can sometimes turn into a needy and neurotic harpy.

Things to avoid:

- Don't burst into tears at a party or social gathering. You may think you are just showing your true self, but they will think 'uh oh, time to move away from this one'. The fact is that people go out to have fun. The last thing they want is a bit of real life bursting their social bubble.

- Don't say yes to every invite just because you can't bear to be alone. Let them see that you have your own life and a bit of backbone and it will keep your credibility high.

- Don't bend backwards to accommodate your friends. If you have planned a date and they want to change it at the last minute, don't rush in and agree to any alternatives. Give them a run for their money. Tell them you are busy on such and such a day. If they think you are desperate to see them and have an empty diary, they may take advantage of you.

- Don't try and win your friends over. They will either like you for who you are, or they aren't worth bothering about. Don't be the kid in the playground, arm outstretched, shouting, 'pick me, pick me!'

- Don't agree to everything people say. If you are in a conversation and your viewpoint is different to everyone else's, stick to it. They will respect you for it.

FANCY A BREAK?

Going on holiday with a buddy could be the perfect way to avoid 'twiddling fingers' syndrome and have a good time. There is nothing better than ten days of sunbathing, drinking tequilas and chatting with a mate. But be careful that you don't rush into booking a holiday just because you've found someone to put suncream on your back.

Here are some of the holiday types to be wary of:
The cry baby: She bursts into tears at the first sign of a problem and will be relying on you to deal with any hiccups you may encounter.

The vacation diva: She takes all morning to get ready for the beach. She has at least five suitcases and your hotel room will be full of her shoe collection and various outfits. When you go out in the evening, she'll insist on dining at the best restaurants and drinking expensive cocktails.

The scrooge: If she's stingy at home, it's bound to be worse on holiday. Do you really want to spend your entire time quibbling over restaurant bills, cups of espresso or just the daily sun lounger? Check out if she tips waiters at home, or always divvys up the bill right down the middle every time.

The moaner: Some people see the negative in everything, which will be magnified when you're going somewhere new. Do you really want a showdown with the holiday rep, just because the room is 'not as big as you would like'. If she's rude to waiters/reception people back home than she's bound to be the same on holiday.

The serial ditcher: She may have come on holiday with you, but she'll ditch you the moment she meets a hot waiter/local/holiday-maker. Loyalty is her big issue and, if she's fickle when she's at home, chances are she won't bat an eyelid when it comes to dumping you in the hotel room.

So, how do you problem-proof your holiday? While it's impossible to plan for every eventuality, you can minimise the risks with a bit of forward thinking.

Here are some tips for having a hassle-free vacation:

- Make sure that you choose the right travelling companion. You want to avoid any mishaps or misunderstandings before you board the flight. Otherwise you could be setting yourself up for two weeks of holiday hell.

- Talk about what you expect beforehand. Set aside a time and place and go through all the things that could cause tension.

- Make sure you are in the same 'money' zone. If she is a high earner and is expecting cordon-bleu dining and expensive days out, then you could find yourself in an embarrassing situation or broke! Let her know what you think the budget should be and see if you are on the same page.

- Agree beforehand whether you pool your money in a holiday kitty or split the bills as they come along.

- Find out if you want to do the same things? If she wants to stay out till dawn and you want to get your beauty sleep you'll have problems. No one wants to be woken up by a party girl stumbling into the room at four in the morning. Find out if she's a sightseer or a beach bum.

- Do the holiday trade off: If you relish hours relaxing in the sun with a couple of poolside Martinis and she's standing over you with a map and a bus timetable, then you are going to be bickering your way through the holiday. Find out whether you could compromise and do both or whether you might benefit from some 'me' time during the day. Often holidays with friends work when you're not stuck together 24/7. After all, you're going to need something to talk about over dinner.

- Do you want to share a room or pay extra for some well-earned privacy? Shared rooms (see wedding section) may be a great idea for saving money, but boy are they stressful. Don't underestimate the power of privacy. Your own space may be particularly important when you're spending so much time with someone else.

~ Chapter Seven ~

OUTTA MY WAY BITCH!

KNOW THE SINGLE SISTERHOOD

THE CATFIGHT

Men play drinking games and have fist fights when they want to prove who is top dog, Women bitch. Like it or not, catty comments and subtle scheming are all part of the female DNA. Remember back at school in the playground, there was always the alpha teenager, the pretty blonde with a posse of male admirers and a gang of girlie followers. All it took was one stare, one put down from the playground princess and you were banished to schoolgirl Siberia. Fast forward thirty-odd years and the female landscape isn't much different. Only this time there are wrinkles, grey hair and expensive handbags. From the passive-aggressive put-downs to the back stabbing and tricky tactics, whenever there are single women competing for a slice of the social pie, there is always a cat-calling, bitch fest waiting to begin. When the stakes are high, such as for getting one up at parties/the beach/ the gym, or even snagging the most eligible bachelor, there is bound to be more scheming than in a room full of politicians at election time.

You would have thought we would be over it by now. As we hit our forties and realise what really matters in life – family, inner feelings and being nice for a start – you might be forgiven for assuming a mature calm would wash over us. Shouldn't we morph into polite, forgiving sisters ready to turn the other cheek rather than turn scarlet with envy and have a full on hissy fit? You've got to be joking! When it comes to dealing with the single sisterhood, you might as well be at a feeding frenzy at the zoo. Trust me, it's a jungle out there, a hotbed of competition with plenty of skulduggery and shameful barbed insults.

So now you're single, are you prepared for the catfight? Think about it. When you were part of a couple, you pretty much got to avoid the bitch fest. After all, if you spent most of your time mooching about the home or out and about with other couples, your world would be pretty much bitch free. Apart from the odd boss bitch or the party whore, you could get on with your day in the knowledge that you were well out of the catfight.

Not anymore. When you are flying solo and competing for hot young himbos or husband number two, you're going to come across the snide sisterhood. These are the nasty women who come in and out of our lives and can cause havoc. If you are determined to make a go of your solo phase, it pays to know how to stay ahead of the pack. Here is the step-by-step guide to help you claw your way to the top:

Are you suffering from 'too nice' syndrome?

Have a look at the following:

- Do people mess you around a lot?

- Do you find yourself always doing what everyone else wants?

- Do you put your needs, desires and life after those of everyone else?

- Are you surrounded by women who tell you what to do?

- Do you try to keep everyone happy all the time?

- Are you always the first to back down from an argument?

- Do you feel selfish if you think about putting yourself first?

If you answered yes to at least three of the above, then you could be just too selfless. We all want to nice. After all, it feels good to like and be liked. Yet, if you are nicer to others than you are too yourself; if you're overly concerned about what other people think, then you may have slipped into 'too anxious to please syndrome'. The trouble is, if we are too nice we can pay the price. Not only can people take advantage of you, you end up putting your own needs on hold and looking after everybody else's needs. Before long you are tired, exhausted and burst into tears just because the postman glared at you.

It's no secret that being alone in midlife can make us feel insecure and as a result we try that bit harder to please people – it's human nature after all. But it's time to toughen up, because sometimes being nice doesn't get you what you want. Even if you feel nervous as a midlife singleton, sometimes it pays to 'suck it up' and get the boxing gloves on.

What to do:
While it would be unrealistic to suggest you turn into a harridan in heels just yet, it is time to get yourself into focus: If you are having a dip in confidence then this section will get you started:

Unleash your inner 'tough nut': Instead of always going along with everyone else. Pause for a minute and think. Say to yourself: What do I want to do? The more you concentrate on how you feel, the more empowered you are.

Have a strong voice: If someone agrees all the time, smiles and nods their head, you either end up asleep or ready to ring their neck. Ditto the ever-smiling pleasant woman who cuts up her cake into little pieces and sips her tea as if she's a timid mouse. We all need some degree of self confidence in order to be an interesting companion. If you find yourself feeling uncomfortable or having a shyness attack, then there are ways to learn how to be assertive.

Start slowly, say something interesting and watch how people respond. More than likely it will be positive, so next time up the ante and say a bit more. Make yourself relax. Tell yourself that if everyone laughs in your face, so what. No one will die, the world won't stop turning on its axis. This kind of thinking frees you up and makes you feel lighter. Hold your head high and don't fidget. Ditto hunched shoulders and hair falling all over the face. Even if you are feeling as if you wished the ground would open up and swallow you, relax, pull your shoulders back and hold your head high. Looking confident will speak volumes.

Don't gabble: When we are nervous we either stay silent or talk at a rate of knots. If you feel yourself going into verbal overdrive, slow your voice down and take a pause. Be calm, avoid raising your voice and look at the people you are talking to.

THE MIDLIFE MAFIA

We women check each other out don't we? Is she slimmer/younger/prettier than me? These are some of the thoughts that pop into our head the minute we are face to face with another woman. We clock each other's shoes/bags/dresses and even each other's friends. Knowing where you are on the success-o-meter is vital in getting ahead.

While men just throw their money around and try to tell the best joke, women compete in far more subtle and deadly ways. It may be that we don't want to compete as such, a lot of us are not unkind, we just want to reassure ourselves. But, and here's the thing, there are women out there who not only want to win, but they want you to lose. So, if you find yourself dealing with the midlife mafia, and there is some deadly one-upmanship afoot, it pays to have a fighting chance!

Here are five ways to bitch up!
Dress to impress. Whether it's a party, dinner or a day at the races, sometimes it pays to look a million dollars. When you look good, you are sending out the message that you take pride in your appearance. Believe me people think twice at pulling a stroke on you. So get out the skyscraper heels, have your hair done and invest in a statement frock. You know it makes sense.

Stay cool calm and collected: Have you noticed how bitchy women never lose control? No matter what happens, they manage to be as cold as ice and as cunning as a fox. So, how do you avoid a melt-down when you're up against a midlife bitch? If you feel yourself going as red as a beetroot, don't be tempted to stomp your feet or cry. Count to ten and calm down. If you think you're going to boil over into a hissy fit, take her aside and shout at her in private. That way you don't end up with egg on your face and your reputation in tatters.

Learn to read their weaknesses: Alpha women always like to sparkle when they are at social functions. Yet sometimes underneath the perfect smile and carefully applied make-up, they may feel just as ragged or self-conscious as the rest of us. Sometimes we just hide our true feelings and fake it. If you spot a woman who has a painted-on smile yet her face looks like thunder, then while she may sound as if she is having a great time, she is probably under strain. Ditto, the woman whose face sags like a deflated soufflé, the instant she thinks no one is looking. People are often not as confident as they try to make out. If you can learn the art of reading the subtext, you will instantly feel more confident and powerful and it feels great.

Create a ring of confidence: By the same token, it pays to ring fence your own emotions. This is not to say you have to spend the rest of your life shielding your vulnerabilities from everyone around you. It simply means don't show your cracks when the sharks are circling! Master the art of aristocratic disdain. By that I don't mean running off and marrying a lord, simply just learn to look as if you're above it all. Giving the impression that you don't care a hoot what other people think. The more self-contained you seem, the more it will engage the emotions of those around you. It will create an air of mystery and power, and soon people will be coming to you.

The dirty look: Learn how to throw your rival a look vile enough to make grown men cry. Then turn to the people around you and smile. 'Daaaahling, haven't seen you in yonks,' you say as you flash her a full-on lip-curling, eyebrow-arching death stare, and watch as your rival shrivels in front of you.

Stand out from the crowd: See an arthouse movie, wear something original or learn an unusual foreign language. By being different you will shine out from the herd and get tongues wagging. Better still cultivate a dirty laugh, practise a sexy walk to show people that you are to be reckoned with.

Watch out for the bitch slap

Of course, while you are honing your bitch skills, it pays to watch out for any bitch slaps that are bound to be coming your way. So, how do you know if you've been stung by a bitch attack? If you walk away from someone and you feel bad inside, yet you can't put your finger on why, chances are someone has invalidated you. Unhappy people will put you down so subtly that you don't know it's happening until you feel curiously depressed or upset.

So to keep you in the loop, here are some bitch slaps to watch out for:

Sweet cyanide: This one is tagged onto the end of what seems at first to be a compliment. 'Julie's a really sweet person,' the bitch will say smiling, 'but...'. Then she launches into an epic long attack about her hair, her manners, her upbringing anything that will make her look as if she should be sent to the Gulag.

The negatron: This bitch makes out she is your friend, then one day you meet her at the bar. Just as you're chatting and joking with everyone, she turns to you and says in a voice reserved for little old grannies, 'Here, let me give you the number of my hairdresser,' and then she rolls her eyes. Beware, this one is jealous of you, and she wants to pull the rug from under your feet so she can step in and shine. Don't fall for her game. Look her right in the eye, pull yourself up to your full height, roll your eyes and laugh. She will get the picture and rush off with her tail between her legs.

Yawn yawn: This bitch comes up to you smiling and asks you about your children/aunt/friend, then just as you start to tell her about your poor aunt Edna and her shingles, she's cut you off in mid sentence and is talking to someone else. Combined with a withering look, it suggests, you are more boring than watching paint dry. Ouch!

The jokes on you: There you are having lunch with a bunch of friends. Bitch turns to you and asks you about your job. Just as you are telling her the ins and outs of publishing/teaching, she laughs and says, 'only asked, didn't want a résumé'. What? You think, confused and dumbstruck, the hurt registering all over your face. Kerching! Game over! She has lobbed a verbal hand grenade right into your lap, and now she is lapping up the fallout.

So, if you are in the middle of bitch territory, here are some catty comments to watch out for:

- Remind me of your age... my mother's looking for someone to complete her reading group.

- What a great voice you have, it sounds just like a foghorn.

- You look great... if the lights were dimmed.

- Lovely top, your nipples stick out like hard peas.

- I have been to some great parties, but this isn't one of them.

- Great dress, it's amazing what you can do with an old tablecloth.

- I wouldn't call her fat, just well rounded

SSSH, HAVE YOU HEARD THE NEWS?

While ruining reputations and spreading false rumours is out and out bitchery, a good old gossip can be good for you. Studies show that having a chinwag with friends increases the level of progesterone, which gets rid of pent up anxiety and stress. And besides, any woman knows that having a good old gossip is not only relaxing, it's great fun too: Just make sure you don't go overboard. Here are the gossip rules:

- Do feel free to bitch and tittle-tattle about celebrities. After all, isn't that why we buy all those trillions of celeb magazines?

- Don't spread a nasty rumour about someone that could hurt them.

- Do discuss people's relationships behind their backs. It's not as if you are bad-mouthing them. But talking about other people is a ways of keeping the social bonds alive – so the scientists say.

- Don't pull someone to shreds who is not there to defend themselves.

- Do discuss the new intern at work. After all, it's not as if you are saying bad stuff. Right?

- Don't write anything down that could be incriminating. It can always come back to haunt you.

HOW TO BE A DIVA HOLLYWOOD WOULD BE PROUD OF

We all love the stories of movie stars demanding their trailers be painted bright blue and fitted with gold carpets. Or, pampered celebrities ordering flunkies to 'take the bubbles out of their coca cola!' When it comes to showing who's top dog, the stars are notorious for behaving like divas on heat. Of course, back on Planet Normal there are enough women who demand special attention and order people around just so they too can feel self important.

A diva will:

- A diva will keep her personal trainer/manicurist and underlings waiting.

- Get others to jump through burning hoops just to please her.

- Floor her opponent with a witty put down and a laugh as throaty as a toad with a sore throat.

- Promise lots and deliver little.

- Have a full-on tantrum a two-year-old would be proud of if someone dares to bring them warm orange juice.

- Make everyone think she is their friend and then bitch about them behind their back.

- Forbid her underlings to sing/talk in her presence.

- Change her mind all the time and watch while everyone scurries around her.

The bitch list

As well as your average diva there are other harridans lurking in the undergrowth? Here are the four main bitches you may come across:

Super bitch

This one takes the bitch to a whole new level. The ultimate predator dressed in Chanel and high heels, she has the strategies of a modern-day Machiavelli and the shadiness of a Columbian drugs dealer. With a glacial smile, she will circle her prey and strike when you least expect it. Charming, sexy and with the presence of a contemporary Alexis Carrington, there is nothing SB won't do to get her own way. Skulduggery and intrigue are her middle name and she can wipe out a rival with a plan that would fox even the CIA. A megalomaniac with a nice hairdo and a pair of scary shoulder pads, she stalks the corridors of power and the salons of the rich. Her goal: world domination, and if you ever get in her way, she'll knock you sideways with a thwack of her nail varnished claw. If you are not skiing in St Moritz or holidaying on a private Caribbean island, you are unlikely to run into this smooth-talking operator. But be careful, there is nothing worse than SB on her way down, she will steal your date, your friends and then she'll come after your soul. Don't even think of taking her on. Avoid at all costs.

Pop princess

She may be as sweet as candyfloss on the outside, but make no mistake, the pop princess is as deadly as any other snide sister. Softly spoken with a voice like velvet, and the face of an angel, her little-girl -lost act is her greatest weapon. Since she was knee-high to a nipper, she's been pulling out the cutesy card to get exactly what she wants. Whether it was a new dolly/pony/someone else's husband, the PP has more tricks up her sleeve than a magician.

'Can I bother you for a few minutes?' she says in a voice as quiet and as humble as a mouse. 'Of course,' you say, putting your arm around her and feeling like a kindly big sister. Don't be fooled.

Once she's laid her honey trap, she'll pour out her troubles for hours on end. She thinks nothing of sobbing down the phone, to get you to come over and spend the evening ministering wine, sympathy and lots of attention. Before you know it, it's midnight, you're tired, wrung out and ready for a week's holiday. Whether she has a snag in her new expensive jumper, her boyfriend hasn't returned her call or she is 'vewwy vewwy' tired, she is only concerned about one person, herself. Then one day when you've abandoned your chores, your children and your daily hygiene, your hair is a mess and she has run you ragged, you finally tell her to get a grip. At that moment PP will turn to you and say in a cheery voice laced with ennui, 'Are you ok, you look really tired? I think it's time you got your act together.' Aware that she has been rumbled, she has no more use for you. She will take you off her friend list, freeze you out of her inner circle and move on to more fertile ground. The next time you find yourself dealing with a PP cut her off before it's too late. Don't spend hours listening to her drone on about her hassles with the plumber. Put the receiver down, never call her again and congratulate yourself on a lucky escape.

The style diva
Found at parties and any other social function, SD wants to be top dog in the 'looks' stakes. Perfectly groomed and wearing the latest designs, the SD competes in Oscar de la Renta and any other cutting-edge designer wear. She will judge everyone by the cut of their out-fit, and whether they know their Louboutins from their Jimmy Choos. If you dare to rock up in anything short of 'this season', or worse bag-gy and saggy, she'll give you a deadly withering look and then turn to fellow SDs and laugh. The best plan of action with this one, is to spot her before she has a chance to get her crimson claws out. Either steer clear, or if she does sidle over, knee boots swaying in the sunshine, look her straight in the eye and say, 'Lovely boots, my mother has a pair just like them.' Bitchy maybe, but she'll be so gob-smacked,

she'll turn on her spiked heels before she realises she's been outwitted by a gal dressed head to toe in last year's Zara.

The bitch boss

You can hear the BB a mile away. Whether she's swearing down the phone at a poor intern, having a tantrum or cursing under her breath, the BB is as unpleasant as a toxic outbreak. She will start the day with pursed lips, stomp down the corridor and think nothing of throwing her Blackberry across the room when something doesn't go her way. Bossy, bullying and known to reduce her employees to fits of tears, the BB is often in a management position so she is bound to get away with her daily fit of desk rage. So while you are popping back the Rennies and calling in sick with stress overload, she just goes on shaming and blaming her co-workers when deadlines are not met and things go wrong. Of course, underneath every blunderbuss is a frightened woman who is scared of being found out. Stressed and most probably not as self-assured as she would like you to believe, your best tack is to say nothing and wait for an opportunity to expose her.

HOW NOT TO BE A SANGRY (SINGLE AND ANGRY)

It's not fair is it? Nice girls finish last and the nasty girls have all the fun. It's enough to make your blood boil. There are a lot of angry singletons out there, and it's no wonder. After all, you may have turned into a middle-aged man hater. You know the feeling. Your ex dumped you for a younger woman; every man under 80 is giving your niece the once over; and you're mistaken for a hat stand.

Maybe you are resentful that life hasn't turned out the way you though it would. After all, did any of us imagine we would be back on the single merry-go-round just as we started our slow slide into crimplene slacks and dodderyness. Maybe you're pissed off that all the good men are taken and those that are left are the old codgers with a bad case of alopecia and wandering-hand syndrome.

Maybe, just maybe, you're sick and tired of taking the rubbish out on your own, putting up the bookshelves and crying yourself to sleep when you're down with the flu. Aaargh!

My own sangry moment happened last year at a posh wedding in Tuscany. I was tanned, toned, sporting honey highlights and wearing my new floaty chiffon number. I felt good. I felt pretty and I was flirting with the best of them. I giggled and tossed back my head as I spoke to a handsome Italian man in his late 50s. As the sun set on the hills, we were a picture of middle-aged happiness, him laughing and me chattering away enthusiastically. Then it happened. Just as I thought we were getting on, just as I pictured him lying on my new pink sofa, he did a double take. A blonde 20-something bimbette with bazooka boobs and pingy-back skin sauntered past and flashed him one of those, 'I-like-what-I-see mega smiles'. He muttered something about getting a drink and before you could say, 'but I want to marry you,' he was off in hot pursuit of a woman young enough to be his daughter. He didn't speak to me for the rest of the weekend. I went from giggly and tipsy to mawkish and inebriated. At one point, I stumbled onto the dance floor and gave an embarrassing rendition of the chicken dance. Apart from a few clumsy bottom grabs and clumsy lunges by some of the older men, I sloped off to my hotel room with a broken shoe and a bruised ego. Since when did even the older men start hating us my inner voice asked? Soon, I was stomping inwardly with rage. Not grumpy as in 'the TV repair man hasn't come' harrumphy way, but angry in an 'it's a really unfair life' way.

And therein lies the rub. Unfair moments will crop up a lot in the re-single's life, so it pays to be clever. In my case, I spent a few weeks resentful and bitter about being over forty and on my own. I whined, I moaned to my friends. I became snappy and stroppy. I had a face of thunder most of the time, and if I did talk to men – I was like a cat when faced with danger – hissing and spitting under my breath. So not good and sooooooo not attractive. In the end a friend took me aside and told me to sweeten up if I didn't want to end up a sad spinster who is eaten by her cats.

So this is what I did

I decided there was no point getting mad anymore. After all, it was making me unhappy. So I decided it was time to turn myself into a 'sappy' (single and happy). I realised that I didn't have to wait for someone or something to turn my life around. I found that I could bring happiness into my life. Learning how to enjoy life and making the most of what you have is the first step to being a fulfilled middlie. And you don't have to make big changes. Small tweaks in the right direction is all it takes from going from sad to sappy. Have a look at our get sappy programme and enjoy!

Ten secrets to being happy

Stop frowning now: If you go around with 'life's a bitch' expression on your face people will feel wary of approaching you. Think of something pleasant the next time you're in a room full of people if you want to be popular. Being grumpy can affect our health, too. Studies have shown that when we think grumpy thoughts we release the stress hormone cortisol into our bloodstream, which dampens our immune system and over a long period can make us ill. And, get this – the body doesn't know whether we are faking a good mood or not. So the next time you feel like falling into a self-pity slump, shake it off and think of something positive. Your body will thank you for it.

Create your own midlife commune: You don't need to be in a relationship to surround yourself with love and close-knit companionship. All you need to do is friend-up. Get hold of old school/college friends, nurture your existing friends and make new friends with like-minded people. Psychologists say that having good close friends who you can trust and share your intimate concerns with is just as good as a year's therapy.

Do something meaningful: Often losing our relationship can create a big heart-shaped hole in our lives. Yet even if you are feeling a bit down, you don't have to be like a member of the walking-wounded brigade. If you want to level off the emptiness, do something that you find meaningful. Whether it's caring for others or doing charity work with children, finding out what makes your heart glad can raise your happiness levels in a matter of weeks.

Do some green exercise: We all know that doing some kind of activity is good for us, but did you know that walking/cycling in green areas – woodland, countryside or your local park can banish the blues and increase our sense of well-being. According to studies, being in nature has a significant impact on how we feel. The combination of Mother Nature, the colours and the sense that there is something bigger than us, puts things into perspective and calms us down.

Be grateful for what you do have: You don't have to thank the universe every morning when you get up, but why not be happy for what you have. A lot of us spend too much time stuck in the trap of the green-eyed monster, envying other people's lives instead of appreciating our own. So, instead of moaning that you can't holiday abroad this year, why not appreciate long walks in the park and the odd weekend away. By expecting less you may find that you are just as happy.

Give 100 per cent: Whether we are mowing the lawn, making dinner or doing a workout routine, if we make an effort-and-a-half, we end up enjoying it more. There is something about doing things well that makes us feel better and more confident.

Don't dwell on past failures: It's comforting to slump into a vat of swirling self pity. 'It's not fair', you say, large glass of wine in hand and big dollopy tears falling on the table. 'I'm such a loooser!' Because, and here's the thing, dwelling on what you did wrong, is a great way to avoid action. If you feel a self-pity moment coming on, stop, give yourself a break and think of something positive to do instead. You'll feel like a happy bunny in no time.

Love the freedom: Instead of moaning about the negatives why not concentrate on all the positives? Instead of worrying about life passing you by and dwelling on your ex, think about all the great things about being single. You have the freedom to do what you want; relax when you want; the chance to grow at your own pace; and start a new life. Free yourself from the thought that you need 'the one' to be happy and start to see this stage in your life as a fun exciting adventure.

QUIZ
How bitchy are you?

1 How often do you find yourself jealous of your friends?
A Never.
B Sometimes.
C Always.

2 Someone tells you a secret. What do you do?
A It's a secret, so no one, not even the dog will know about it.
B Vow to keep schtum but find yourself telling a few of your closest friends.
C You're on the phone before you can say sssh it's a secret, and by noon you have told everyone you know.

3 You're at a party and your friend is talking to a man you find attractive. Do you?
A Wish her luck and back off.
B Wish her luck but wait around in case there is no chemistry between them.
C Sidle up and with your sweetest smile ask her how her 'thing' is.

4 You go to a dinner party and another woman is wearing the same trouser suit. What do you do?
A Have a good laugh about it, and compliment her on her taste.
B Smile, but sit as far away as possible.

C Spill your glass of white wine all over her. Sorry.

**5 A friend tells you something embarrassing about herself.
Do you?**
A Listen to her and give her good friendly advice.
B Listen to her for a bit and then make your excuses and leave.
C Pretend you are ooooh sooo concerned and then tell everyone about it later.

6 You have an argument with a friend. What do you do?
A Apologise and make up.
B You both apologise and have a laugh.
C You know you are in the wrong, but you go on the attack anyway.

7 A junior colleague at work does something wrong. Do you?
A Spend a while telling her how to correct her mistakes.
B Say nothing and let her find out for herself.
C Scream and shout and humiliate her in front of the entire office.

8 How would your friends describe you?
A Really nice, would do anything for anyone. A bit of a pushover really.
B Keeps herself to herself but is a sound member of the gang.
C Very, very scary.

9 You are at a restaurant and the food arrives cold. Do you?
A Say nothing. Anything for a quiet life.
B Speak calmly and politely and ask the waiter to heat it up.
C Shout and scream and tell the waiter that he is an incompetent oaf.

10 You find out that there is a promotion at work. Do you?
A Think you'll never get it – nothing good ever happens to you.
B Put in some really hard work and let the best man win.
C Sabotage the other woman's chances. You really want this job.

How did you score?

Mostly As – You are so nice, you might as well be made of sugar. While everyone around you may benefit from your generosity, if you put others before yourself too often, people will start to see you as a pushover and know that they can get the better of you.

Mostly Bs – You are self-assured and fair-minded. For you, justice and doing the right thing are up there on your to-be list. Sometimes it pays to be a bit emotional, after all if you're rational all the time, aren't you just ignoring your own feelings?

Mostly Cs – No one, but no one gets the better of you. Scarier than a Piranha in heels, and with a trust factor of zero, you make sure you're always on top. While you may get your own way, people will soon start to avoid you unless you tone down the bitch dial.

~ Chapter Eight ~

THE LOVE JUNGLE

THE ART OF MIDLIFE DATING

SHOCK OF THE NEW

The party was hotting up nicely. Holding a glass of bubbly, I walzed across the room and flashed a mega-watt smile at the stranger by the bar . Before you could say, 'How do you do', I had planted a wet kiss on his cheek and dragged him onto the dance floor for a spot of disco dancing. It was on my first date since my break-up and things hadn't gone as planned.

It is not surprising, that after being with someone for what seems like a life time, finding yourself back in the dating game can be a bit nerve-racking. In my case, that meant a lot of Dutch courage and stern telling off by my date. Whether you go the 'I will-make-a-fool-of-myself' route or just stay at home and knit jumpers, dating in your forties can seem like a bit of a struggle.

The older we get, the more set in our ways we become and less able to imagine meeting our dream man number two. Not only that, post 40 it's more difficult to meet interesting new people in the traditional way, aka parties and through friends.

Then there is the fact that for the midlife singleteer, modern dating is a very different ball game to the traditional style of boy meets girl. Nowadays, what with virtual flirting, sexting – romance by app and all the other techi ways to find love, it's not surprising that the midlife singleton can find it hard to get a handle on the latest dating rules. I mean when everyone else is talking about text dating, BBMing and uploading your best bikini-fit photo, you could be forgiven for collapsing in a fit of tears and running home to mum.

And let us not forget the age factor. Gone are the days when we could rely on perfect flesh and dresses the size of a hankie to acquire a mate. Now, as we check out our wrinkles and wobbly bits, we ask ourselves, 'What's the competition like?'

How to deal with 20-something jail bait

It's a romantic free-for-all out there, and when it comes to finding a man it's every woman for herself. There are those who would say older women have the thin end of the romantic edge. Just look at all those pneumatic 25-year-olds with their peachy behinds and their glossy, swishy hair. However, not everything is quite so simple. Have a look at these differences:

We:

- Know ourselves and nothing is going to phase us now.

- We have lived, loved and come through the other side with flying colours. Beat that!

- We are honest about who we are and what we want.

- We have learnt to be kind and considerate and to understand a man's failings.

- We are more experienced in bed even if we have more wobbly bits.

They:

- Will be constantly twittering/texting/facebooking their friends with a minute-by-minute update of their love lives.

- Treat a date like an interview. How much does he earn? Does he want more kids? It's enough to have him running into the arms of a re-single before you can say pass the pre-nup!

- Will constantly check themselves out in windows and mirrors – they're so vain and insecure.

- Go on silly eat-a-cabbage-a-day diets that will infuriate men.

- Are as fickle as a leaf blowing in the wind. In love one minute, out on the razzle the next.

WADDYA WANT?

But then, maybe we should forget about the hot young bimbettes and concentrate on what we want. For a start dating in midlife is a lot different to our younger years. Not only are we different to when we were younger, but we are looking for different things in a prospective partner. Gone is the search for the perfect hairdo and the abs of an athlete. Instead of sighing over the glamorous banker with the smart suit and the bank account to match, as we get older and wiser, we are drawn to someone who's going to make an interesting, kind companion. By the same token, not all men want the 20-something arm candy dripping off their arm. They, too, want to meet someone who they can relate to and have an interesting time with. So, it pays to silence the inner critic and just see what happens.

Which brings me to my next point. At what age does a woman realise her pool of potential suitors is shrinking faster than Venice on a wet day, and decide to lower her expectations? After all, if we all want the same guy: Mr solvent with a six pack, a porsche and a condo in the country, then chances are he's going to have all the choice. So, as we hit our 40s, it pays to tweak our romantic spec.

The first thing to consider are the non-negotiables. These are the things in a man that you will not tolerate even if he looks like Harrison Ford with a pay packet to match. Your deal breakers could be someone who flirts like Casanova, lies to you or is really mean with the finances. It could be someone who insists on keeping his house as tidy as a hospital ward or is as grubby and messy as a vagrant. Once you've worked these out, it pays to put them in an email and send it to yourself. That way you'll always have a record to remind you.

The next step is to think of the things that you are not fond of, but hey, you're going to learn to love:

- Makes funny clicking noises while making love.

- Collects model cars and loves Scalextric.

- Wears funny high-waisted corduroy trousers.

- Slurps when drinking tea.

- Has a paunch.

- Is bald.

After a while, by allowing your prospective partner a little more slack you will slowly revise your 'man-plate'. The point of the exercise is not so that you say yes to the first bespeckled male that offers you a drink, but it is a way to open up the possibilities of someone who may not tick all the boxes but is a person you could fall in love with anyway.

THE MIDLIFE DATING PLAN

The next question is this: what are your relationship expectations? Chances are after a nasty break-up, you may simply want to flirt and date for fun. The 'no-strings-attached' fling is not so terrible and is a great way to boost a crushed ego. After all, there is nothing so beautifying and exhilarating than knowing that a) someone finds you attractive, and b) you've still got it going on sister! Phew!

On the other hand – you may be ready for a serious relationship. Whatever you choose, make sure your prospective date is on the same romantic page. You don't want a cling-on who declares his love on date three just as you're moving on to the architect you met at your cousin's party.

Get the dating ball rolling

Once you've realised what you want, it's time to actually get out there and meet some men. Ok, so no one said it was going to be easy. Dating is a bit like going for interviews only the job spec is a little more vague. All those pre-date nerves, the manic date prep and the 'does-he-like-me?' angst are all part of the package. The point is, if you don't do the dating bit, you are never going to get to the warm, comfy relationship part either. Dating is a numbers game, the more people you meet, the more chances you have of meeting 'the one'. So while it may seem worse than having your teeth pulled out, and it may seem oh so tempting to stay resolutely stuck in your old habits, why not make an effort to get in the game?

If you are a bit rusty on the dating front here are some dating rules to get you started:

Get out of your comfort zone: Start taking action. Factor in a man-meeting opportunity at least once a week. For a start it could be signing up to a new man-friendly evening class. It could facebooking your friends to find out if there are any fellow singles. Anything that starts the dating ball rolling is positive.

Ditch the romantic baggage: This can be difficult because by the time you hit 40 you will have had your heart broken and you will have broken a few hearts yourself. You may have betrayed and suffered betrayals, all of which have the potential to give us more baggage than an airport carousel. And when it comes to dating, if you don't leave the resentments and pain in the past, you could end up having one glass of Chardonnay too many and pouring out your post-divorce angst to your hapless date.

Be fun and flirty: Dating success depends on cultivating a carefree attitude that is jolly with a touch of glamour. Lighten up and keep conversation fun and flirty. It's early days after all and you want to excite his imagination not bore him to death. Don't dwell on the 'I've-got-a-lot-on-my-plate' realities as full on frankness is about as sexy as arranging a mortgage. Ditto any mention of the ex. He doesn't want to know all about how Mr so and so was a cad with a bad hairdo when he is sipping eau de romance with you. Keep his attention focused on you and show him just how much fun you can be. If he does want to probe, gloss over uncomfortable facts, you don't need to tell him that you've been in therapy for three months. The trick is to edit and re-edit. And yes, you are allowed to tell a few white lies – 'Oh of course we get on', (when speaking of the ex) and 'yes I luuurve my job'. Little fibs after all, are part of the midlifer's dating arsenal. And there's an-other reason why you should only show your good side early on. The more you present positive 'you', the more confident and happy you appear, and the more people will respond favourably to you, which in turn will make you feel happier.

Don't be too cool to care: While trying hard to please will be as obvi-ous as a Belisha beacon, being overly cool and dismissive can go against you in the love stakes. Men want a woman who has her own life, but they love to think that you need them a tinsy bit. If you are the 'I'll hail my own taxi', or 'I insist on going Dutch on the first date', kinda girl, then you may scare men off. When I first started re-dating, a friend of mine took me aside and said, 'You know what your problem is, Kate? You act like one of the boys', and he was right. I was so scared of looking like that sad single stereotype that I developed a too-cool-to-care persona that was putting men off. Don't hold back from show-ing a man that you like him. The truth is, men are no good at reading the micro expressions you emit. Just because you flashed him a half smile when you walked in the room, doesn't mean that he has put you on his 'she-fancies-me list'. In an effort to safeguard your dating ego, you may be letting one of the good guys go. While grabbing him and giving him a Hollywood kiss before you've even got his last name is may have him running for the hills, there are ways to signal how you feel without having to declare your hand:

Do be warm: Very, very warm. All that edgy, 'like hey, I'm so way out', behaviour really is for young women with tousled just-got-out-of-bed hair, leather jackets and skinny jeans. You're in your 40s for Christ's sake. There's a lot to be said for being a really warm, happy and engaging person.

Don't flirt with his friends: Manic hair flicking and eyelash fluttering with his best bud from college is a sure fire seduction technique – when you're sixteen! Get a grip. We're in our 40s. Making your prospective date jealous by giving out to his friends is just, well, tacky. It will probably backfire anyway. If he thinks you are not that interested in him, he's more than likely to find the first girl in the room and give her the gold star treatment. Then, there you are talking about the NASDAQ with a bunch of blokes from the city, while the man of your dreams is getting flirty elsewhere.

Do laugh a lot: There is nothing men like more than a girl who can have fun. I know, you would have thought they would appreciate your deep and serious side, but according to scientists a laughing, giggling female is dating gold dust.

Do leave for a few minutes: Ask a friend to watch if he checks you out when you go to the ladies. If he doesn't give you the once up and down as you totter across the room, then I'm sorry but he's not as into you as you thought. Also, go and 'take a call'. Not only will this say, I have friends, it will also give him time to miss you. Don't stay away too long though, he may get bored and look for fresh prey.

Mix 'em up: While you should let him know you like him, don't make it too easy. Mix up the messages. At some point in the conversation

155

turn away and look into the middle distance. Don't worry he won't run off and talk to the ice sculpture. When we mix the signals it creates a bit of tension, which is sexy. The more distant you are, the more it engages his emotions. Make him work for you!

Do lean in: I am not suggesting you fall into his arms and send his glass of beer spinning out of his hand. Just lean gently in towards him. He won't know it, but you are creating a warm intimate space that will fast-track your bonding process.

Don't stand there like a bricky chewing gum: While a bit of boyish charm never goes amiss – too much girliness can become cloying – looking distinctly mannish is a turn off. Be delicate and chatty, pull your hair back while telling him a risqué story – the combination of boy/girl erotica is a big turn on.

Look hot to trot: First impressions count for a lot. The way you come across, dress and carry yourself are all part of your appeal. A month ago I went to a party in a bit-too-short, low-cut dress. It took all of five minutes to realise that I looked like Britney Spears while the other women were working the cool and chic look. One cannot emphasise it enough; too much flesh on display has more than a whiff of desperado.

Don't be a jungle animal: The same is true of leopard-print and leather jackets or trousers. Trying to look racy over 30 simply makes you look older. At the other extreme anything mid-calf, especially when teamed with court shoes, can look dowdy and librarianish. Choose clothes that enhance your personal appeal. Work out what flatters your shape and skin tone and develop your own style. You can wear skyscraper heels – only not with a skirt that resembles a belt. Basically, by wearing what makes you feel at ease, you will feel good and radiate confidence.

Get a sharking buddy: If you feel nervous about going out on the hunt alone, then why not find a sharking buddy. This is a new single gal pal or a friend who is in the similar position as you:

The pros:

- It's good to have someone to laugh with after you've been out. And to have the hankies at the ready when the going gets tough.

- There's always someone to tell you that you have spinach in your teeth or a glob of mascara in your eye.

- It's a two-way street. She will boost your confidence if you have a set back and you will do the same for hers.

- There is nothing men like more than seeing two girls having a good time. For a start it shows a) you have friends, and b) how much fun you are. A win-win situation.

- You can develop a dating strategy. If you are shy, she can be the front man and you can come in after she has warmed up the atmosphere.

A few things to bear in mind:
If you do get a sharking buddy, it pays to be on the same attraction level. There is nothing worse than going out on the pull with the skinny rock chick who gets all the attention. You will feel plain and ugly by comparison and your confidence will plummet faster than the NASDAQ on a bad day. Ditto a sharking buddy who is a lot younger than you. Why would you do it to yourself?

Plus, it's useful if you have different ideas about your potential partner. My dating pal loved the tortured artist type with Byronesque curls and a skinny physique. I, on the other hand, wanted someone serious and a cross between Gerard Depardieu and Christopher Plummer. See. Not so similar.

Sex in the city

Where to meet men

The first rule when out sharking is to familiarise yourself with places that have pick-up potential. In other words, maximise your opportunities for meeting men and you are more likely to find Mr Right.

Gallery openings/first nights: These are glamorous, fun and an opportunity to dress up and flirt. With some clever repartee and a strong line in introducing yourself (see the buddy chapter) you can make contacts, meet arty types and still be in bed by 10 pm. (most openings start at 6.30 pm and are over by 9 pm).

International flights: Whether you bond over coffee in the airport lounge or you make sweet talk over the in-flight food service, meeting someone on a flight is a convenient way to hook up. For a start, you don't have to initiate the conversation – you are sitting right next to him – and if you dress to impress you might even get upgraded to first class and meet the businessman of your dreams.

In the rain: A summer downpour has all the hallmarks of a Hollywood romance – well if it worked for Rock Hudson and Doris Day then it can work for you too. There is the sheltering-under-the-shop-awning moment when you strike up conversation and run for cover at the nearest bar. Similarly, there is the 'I'm-going-to-offer-to-share-my-umbrella-with-that-handsome-guy' moment. It makes bad weather sexy!

Talks and lectures: This one is educational and full of pull potential. There are lots of organisations that hold interesting debates and lectures at halls around the city. Find one that has a topic that suits you and rock up. Check out who is there and casually sit next to someone who is potentially interesting. But don't worry if you are seated next to an old couple in their dotage – these events tend to have coffee intervals and a question time afterwards.

The gym: Check out the timetable and attend as many male-oriented classes as possible. That means that circuit training, boxercise and aerobic yoga are in, zumba and legs, bums and tums are out.

At the office: A lot of people frown on office romance, but really I say maximise all your chances. If you work for a big organisation there will be a steady stream of new personnel every week. Keep your eyes open for potential conversation openers and meet and greet.

The supermarket: While the two-for-ones and maxi packs are strictly family fare, if you check out the deli counter, the wine store and easy-cook sections you are bound to find some bachelors walking the aisles. Have a look in his basket if there are flowers, lots of cakes and chocolate, abort. Conversely, if he has a bottle of Vodka and a stack of ready-made meals: attack!

The race track: If there is one place that has the potent whiff of testosterone, it has to be the dog/horse race track. Think of all those pumped-up punters placing their bets and waiting for the win. Go to the bookies and play the girlie card. Ask a handsome punter how to do a 'three-way bet'. He'll love to show off his knowledge and if you're dressed up, he's more than likely to offer you a drink at the members' bar. Result!

The hotel bar: Hotel bars are a bit of a double-edged sword. On the one hand, all those international travellers mean a steady stream of switched-on guys. On the other hand, what are you doing in a hotel bar at this time of night? Tricky one. Either pretend you are staying at the hotel (if he's a gentleman he won't ask to come back to your room). Or, book a mid-week break (room rates are much cheaper on weekdays than on Saturday and Sunday) and take advantage of the breakfast-time pulling potential as well.

Woodwork class: I know, are you really going to sit through all that blah blah about sawing wood just to get a date? My advice is this: Check out some of the more male-friendly evening classes and give them a whirl. You only have to go to a couple of sessions (ask to sit in before you sign up), learn some car maintenance lingo and land yourself a handyman/boyfriend before you can say, 'pass me the car jack'.

Online dating

While meeting a man in three-dimensional reality, aka, the traditional route has lots to recommend it, why not have a side order of cyber love just in case?

Nowadays there are infinite more possibilities on offer. Whether you will only consider men over six foot or you're more than happy dating older men, there is an online dating site out there for you. Gone are the days when only the hapless losers and weird men signed up. In today's busy world, a lot of people don't have the time for endless meetings in bars and have turned to the internet to find a partner.

What to do:

Do some research: Internet dating does cost money, so don't sign up to the first site you come across. Check a few out and make a discerned choice. If you want to have the romantic edge go for one of those over-50s dating sites and enjoy being one of the younger members. Or, if you prefer the more guided route, there are sites out there with questionnaires and other ways to match you with a range of men who come close to your requirements.

Don't give up: As we get older, there are fewer men in our pool. Be patient. When I started on a dating site, the only men who seemed interested in me were lorry drivers with dodgy haircuts. And although I never found love online, I did finally meet some decent men. Remember, you have to date a lot of digi-frogs before you meet your prince.

Do get a good profile picture: Now you are over 40 it pays to show yourself in the best possible light. Don't just get out the iPhone and click. Ask a friend to do a series of pictures showing you in different situations: 'This is me at a party' has the subtext, 'aren't I fun?' Then there is the 'me with a group of friends', subtext for 'I am a warm individual who everyone likes'. I would draw the line at the sexy shots, 'me on the beach in a micro-kini' shot, or worse, the choreographed lying-on-the-bed-in-lacy-underwear/sex-kitten pose, all of which are wrong on so many levels. For a start let him work to see your figure, and secondly have some dignity and wrap up girl.

Don't lie: Shaving off a few years on your profile is likely to backfire. If you start to date, you are caught in a lie. If you tell him, he'll think he can't trust you and maybe he'll leave. If you don't tell him, he'll find out one day – like when you go on holiday and he takes a sneaky peak at your passport. Chances are, he'll feel a little conned. He may forgive you and he may not. Do you really want to take that chance? Ditto putting photos up of you when you were younger. Again, it's disingenuous and when you rock up with a double chin and bit of middle-aged spread he'll feel cheated and make a run for it. Be honest. It's always the best policy.

Speed dating

A word on speed dating. It's quick and relatively painless. You get to say the same thing to a variety of men and slowly perfect your pitch for future dating. Try different techniques: if you see their eyes closing and their mouths dropping when you mention you speak four languages, switch to fluttering eyelids and talking about home economics. It doesn't harm anyone and is a relatively inexpensive way to meet prospective dates. And there are tons of speed-dating events around nowadays. A warning though: as a midlifer, it pays to go for the upper -age group variety. I once went to a 25–55 event and found most of the women there were young enough to be my niece.

THE FIRST DATE

Ok, so you've dated online till your eyes ache, you have partied with the best of them, and it's finally paid off. You've met someone. You've ex-changed numbers/email addresses and you've arranged the first date.

It wouldn't matter if you were the president of the free world or a skydiving champion, there is nothing scarier than preparing for the first romantic meeting with a man you like/fancy/think you might fall in love with. For a start, it's loaded with expectations and the potential for gaffes. You may end up wishing you were at home with a cup of camomile tea rather than sitting with him, or you may fall head over heels and tell him you've fallen in love! So, how do you make sure that your first encounter is a fun night out rather than a resounding flop?

Here are some first date tips:

Dress to thrill: You want to be understated, a bit flirty and sexy without advertising that you are up for it. That means whatever you do, don't flash too much flesh. A figure-hugging black or red dress will get his pulse rate up without slipping over into hooker territory. Remember, if you are displaying cleavage go easy on the hem length. The golden rule of midlife dressing is one erogenous zone at a time please. Wear a cute cardi over the top, or a jacket to smarten up the outfit and help keep you warm as the evening draws on. There's nothing worse than goose bumps and wishing you were wrapped in a duvet as you are trying to be your sparkly witty self.

Don't have a radical makeover just before the date: You may be tempt-ed to overhaul your image of the new hair cut, new me type. If it goes wrong and you end up looking a mess, you'll feel awful and end up wearing a beanie hat. Besides, he liked how you looked otherwise he wouldn't have asked you on a date. If it works, don't change it.

Don't over do the alcohol beforehand: Sure, have a glass of Dutch courage before you set off to calm pre-date nerves, but if you get stuck into the vino blanco just before the date and arrive tiddly, you're not only sending out the message that you're nervous, you'll probably trip over the waiter and fall headlong into the restaurant.

Take a cab: No woman wants to arrive hot and flustered, with rivulets of mascara running down her cheeks and a snag in her tights, just because she had to negotiate the subway rush hour in a posh frock and high heels.

Arrive at least ten minutes late: That way you can do a quick 'once over' as you walk into the restaurant, and hopefully he'll have had time to get you a welcome drink.

Set the tone by giving him a polite kiss on the cheek and a warm smile.

Chances are you'll get along splendidly. However, the following should raise red flags for you and indicate it's time to leave.

It's time to dump your date when:

- He spends the whole date ogling a group of 20-something girlies.

- He is rude to the waiter/receptionist/other guests.

- He is rude to you.

- He makes obnoxious comments, such as 'I don't like fat/ ugly people'.

- He spends the whole date droning on about his ex.

- He punches the man at the next table just because he was staring at you.

- He is so boring you find the menu more interesting.

- He gets drunk and starts feeling you up or stroking your back. A gentleman never touches on the first date.

How to end a successful first date

So, you felt like you had known him for ages. You have the same taste in films/holidays and soft furnishings. You love the way his eyes crinkle and you really want to see him again. How do you leave the date? Is it a polite kiss on the cheek with a follow-up text, or are you on for a bit of tonsil hockey?

I don't care what you say, the first kiss after a date is as terrifying at 45 as it was when you first snogged Jimmy in second grade. After all, it's a trailer for what's going to come – so it pays to get it right.

Picture the scene. You are standing at your doorway and he is telling you how much he enjoyed the date. Do you give him the green light and lean in or say, 'ummm yeah ok thank you', and slam the door in his face? No you don't.

Here is the kissing countdown:

- Relax your features and compose yourself.

- Turn to face him and smile.

- Move in leaning your face towards his.

- If he doesn't take the hint, pull you towards him and give you a Hollywood smooch, take the initiative.

- Give him a soft, gentle kiss on the cheek and say good night. Job done. Sweet dreams.

Hang on a minute!
What about if he asks to come upstairs? From his point of view he's coming up if he can. But from your point of view, big mistake! Unless you're prepared for the hook up and leave, aka the one-night stand, then stay in control. Let me explain. Even if you are as sex-starved as a man without water in the Gobi desert, it really doesn't pay to put out on the first date. Forget all this nonsense about men not caring whether you have a sex swing in your bedroom or you wear socks in bed. Believe me they care. Men have not changed that much. If you put out after a few hours in their company, in the back of their mind just above the football scores and their bank balance is the niggling doubt. It goes like this, 'Mmm, so she slept with me on the first date. Does that means she sleeps with every man on the first date?' And before you can say, 'but I love you madly', you may be relegated to the fun, but a bit-too-easy list. My advice is this: If you like him then leave him wanting more. Simple.

Whatever you do. Whether you are making him eggs over easy the next morning or you left him on the doorstep, a good encounter will end with a text from him and a promise of things to come.

~ Chapter Nine ~

LEAVING THE TOILET
SEAT UP

ALL ABOUT THE MAN

So what are men all about anyway? What, you mean you've got half-way through your life and you don't know? Well it sure as heck took me a long time to work out how the other half works. Questions such as, why do men always leave the toilet-up/ balance beer mats on their nose/climb really high mountains hurtle through our minds leaving us perplexed and wondering whether we should laugh or cry. The truth is, men are vastly different from women in so many ways.

Things you should know about men (which you probably do already). They:

- Are much noisier than women. This is for two reasons: Firstly they want to announce their presence above all the other men – it's the human equivalent of the mare who de-posits his dung on top of his rivals to make sure his smell is the most potent, and secondly because there is no sweeter noise than the sound of their booming voice.

- Are much smellier than women. Again, testosterone (the male hormone) is what gives men that potent, whiffy smell you get in the mornings before you fling open the windows and gasp for a lung full of fresh air. Plus, if left to their own devices, your average guy is not as hygiene-conscious as your average female. You only have to think skid-mark man, pongy socks man, to get some idea of how some things are way down on their to-do list.

- Will balance beer mats on their nose/buy the most expen-sive bottle of champagne in an effort to get your attention. And the older they get, the more they show off. As their pecs morph into droopy man boobs and their stomachs fill out like a medicine ball, they up the ante. Your average single middle-aged man will buy a Harley/Porsche/get a hair transplant/wear a ridiculously trendy shirt all to say, 'look at me, me, me'.

- Will climb mountains in sub-zero temperatures and suffer frostbite all in the name of 'a challenge'. But God forbid you ask them to take the trash out in the cold. They will shiver and moan until you step out into the freezing cold in your nightie and a pair of Ugg boots.

- Like to behave badly and then lie about it.

- Will offer advice when all we want is some TLC and sympathy.

- Will go to the supermarket for essentials and return with a six pack of beer and an oven-ready pizza.

- Snore in bed, stomp around the room in the middle of the night, and if that isn't bad enough they always steal the duvet.

- Tend to be averse to washing socks/picking up towels and any other chore that women tell them to do.

- When he says he has a good sense of humour, he means you laugh at his jokes. Period.

- Reach middle age and start flirting with shop assistants/ waitresses/young librarians, any woman, in fact, who will smile back at them and shore up their flagging ego.

- Are never wrong. Right?

- Don't age, they just mature. Or so they keep telling us.

- Have opinions. You are just opinionated.

- Would rather end up in a ditch than ask directions.

Men are not only the polar opposite of women, they are also different from each other. Do you always find yourself dating/marrying the wrong men? The trouble is, the more toxic a man is, the more charming he will be to you. Have a look at who's who in our Hall of Man-famy and watch out for the rotters.

The commitment phobe

This predator is a rotter with a capital 'R'. A charming man about town, he knows his way around the female heart. After all, he has been talking to women since he met his first girlfriend in St Tropez. All his friends are female and he can often be found dispensing little pearls of wisdom as an honorary member of the 'girls lunch'. The trouble begins when you fall for his charms and start to take him seriously. At first he will shower you with compliments and treat you like a princess, until you ask a fatal question. 'So where is this relationship going?' you ask one day after six months of dates that are leading nowhere. He will fall silent and nearly choke on his lobster bisque. Inwardly he is planning his exit. 'Terrible traffic jam', he'll mutter when he's late for dinner the following week. Suddenly he'll be up at the crack of dawn to 'go to a meeting', subtext he wants to avoid breakfast with you. In short the commitment phobe has no intention of taking the relationship onto the next level. Cull immediately!

The signs
- He will keep secrets from you. He doesn't tell you where he's going. He has no intention of settling down.

- He loves women. Whether they are his friends/colleagues or gym buddies, you name it, he hangs out with the girls.

- He doesn't introduce you to his mates. Well, he has no intention of making you a permanent fixture in his life

How to handle
Whatever you do, don't become clingy unless you want to drive him away as quick as a man fleeing from a burning building. If he pulls back, simply pull back further. Can't make your mother's Sunday lunch, don't worry invite someone else, preferably a much younger man who you've fancied for ages. The more unavailable you are, the more he will come running. Don't waste too much time on this one. Play him at his own game for a while and then make sure you leave first.

The love rat

With the smile of George Clooney, the elegance of James Bond and the charisma of a modern-day Errol Flynn, the love rat is a master of seduction. Handsome and sexy in his open-necked shirt and his Gucci loafers, he is a soignée asset at any party. One part boyish charm, one part playful sex appeal and just a little dash of danger, he is a hard man to resist. He will flatter and flirt and make any nouveau divorcee feel as if she is a 16-year-old girl again. Beware, the love rat is out to get what he can and has zero regard for your feelings. His desire for instant gratification and the sport of it all are what drives this animal. He is so hard to resist, that the only way you know you've been had is the empty space in your bed.

The signs
- He will come on as strong as an Exocet missile and will aim straight at your heart.

- He will concentrate all his energy on you, and make you

feel as if you are the most beautiful and intelligent woman in the world.

- He is touchy-feely from the moment he strikes up conversation in the hotel lobby. He pulls a hair from your face and you are smitten. Love rat is an opportunist and when he has had his way, he will move on to feast off another victim.

How to handle
Whatever you do, don't fall under his spell. Unless you are up for a night of passion – in which case 'Go gurrl', as love rat is usually an exciting and adventurous lover – then you are better off waiting. If he starts to put the pressure on, look him in the eyes and say in your sweetest voice, 'I think we should get to know each other first', then watch as he makes a dash for the exit.

The mummy's boy

With a mother hovering over his every move from the year dot, the mummy's boy is like a new born blinking into the sunlight of adulthood. In other words, he is a gurgling, burping child-adult. Brought up to think he is the most wonderful thing since sliced bread, mummy's boy thinks that women were made to pick up his laundry, make his food and feed his ego. Since his mommy bought him the new bike/toy car and the town house, mummy's boy is used to getting his own way. Be careful if you find yourself in a relationship with this one. One false move and he will have a full-on temper tantrum that would put a two-year-old to shame.

The signs
- He will play the little boy act the moment he meets you and unleash your inner mommy.

- Watch out for the, 'I was neglected/misunderstood/bullied' stories. They are probably false and designed to press your sympathy buttons.

- He may even go for the rounded-shoulders-bowed-head-poor-little-me body language to trick you into feeling for him.

How to handle

At first the affectionate mummy's boy can seem such a cutie, especially if your ex was a controlling son-of-a-bitch. But after you've listened to his stories, booked his appointment with the doctor, and bought his special medicine (he 'suffers such allergies', his mother tells you in that cloying way of hers) you may find you are worn out. Let him know that you are not there to look after him. Ask him to do some things for you and if he looks at you as if you are mad, then send him back to his mom where he belongs.

The iron man

This one will eat super-sized burgers for breakfast and protein drinks for snacks. With arms that would put Popeye to shame and abs you could sharpen a knife on, The iron man is about power and strength. Fatigue is for wimps, man! A cross between Conan the Barbarian and Gunga Din, iron man likes to think of himself as part warrior part human Corinthian Column. This animal will literally swing from the chandelier and catch you in his enormous arms. Unlike the love rat, iron man has about as much romantic savoir faire as a 5 kg dumbbell.

The signs
- Obsessed with bulking up and cutting down on trans fast, he won't even notice if your bum looks big. He's too busy checking his own.

- Will turn up on a date in his Storm Fly airtex jacket and running leggings, and spend the entire time checking out his biceps in the mirror.

- Will order the biggest T-bone steak and forget you're even there.

How to handle
If you are a fellow sports obsessive, you can bond over repetitions and squat lunges. Otherwise, there are simply not enough hours in the day to waste on a man who is more interested in his BMI index than the new dress you just bought.

The male chauvinist pig (MSP)

Stuck somewhere in the past, the MSP really does believe that women are the second sex. For him, the male is supreme and women are way down the food chain. It's not that he's cruel or even a sadist, it's simply that women are fine as long as they know their place – preferably the kitchen! Opinionated and gruff, the MSP loves to throw his weight around, in the boardroom, the bedroom and in the bar. As far as he's concerned, it's a man's world, and quite frankly you are lucky to be in it. Up at 6 am with a conference call over breakfast, and an appointment with his trainer at seven, MSP likes to be busy and active. Scratch the surface of your average MSP and you'll find a quivering mass of confusion. Basically, he is so terrified of women, he would rather crush you to death than let you rule him.

The signs:

- Can often be found at the bar/football/races. Basically any place where there are lots of men and he can feel safe in the fug of testosterone.

- He will look after you, as long as you know your place.

- Will tell you there can be only one captain of the ship. And you know who that is.

How to handle

If you want a man who protects and provides then the MSP is for you. Only don't be surprised if he expects you to run around after his needs. You are a woman after all, dammit! Bat your eyelids and look sweet if you want to get your own way. If you want something done, let him think it's his idea or simply go with the flow. There is no other way. If you challenge him, if you box him into a corner, he'll feel like a humiliated little boy and he'll never forgive you for unmasking him.

The control freak (CF)

The control freak comes across as a strong, powerful alpha male with as much prowess as a lion on the hunt. He looks like a good bet on paper, what with his Gold Amex, high-flying career and condo in the Hamptons. At first it's such a refreshing change to be with someone who seems so capable, so… well, strong. He'll book the best restaurant, organise the weekends away, choose the most expensive outfit for you and all you have to do is sit back and look pretty. But beware, behind his capable persona lies a manipulative bully who wants to control you at all costs. Unlike the true alpha who has integrity and humanity, the control freak is one of the most toxic creatures.

The signs:

- He tells you what to wear, who to see and where to go. The CF wants to dictate every aspect of your life.

- He will monitor your calls and pester you with emails. In short, he'll do what it takes to keep you under surveillance.

- He will explode into a terrifying rage if you disobey his orders. Indeed, underlying his every argument is the message that if you don't do what he wants you will be punished.

- He won't let you load the dishwasher/cook/work the remote. He is hijacking control over the domestic concerns.

How to handle

If you find yourself dating a CF the best thing is to leave right now! There is nothing else for it, unless you want to become a timid shadow of your former self.

The ageing rock star (ARS)

With more tattoos than a fairground worker and a penchant for vintage leather jackets, the ARS is stuck resolutely in the past. While he thinks he is the stuff of Hollywood dreams, he is more strolling bones than Jumpin' Jack Flash. Only don't tell him I said so. From his badly dyed hair, perma tan and smoothed-out botoxed forehead, the ARS is a bit like David Hasselhoff with a guitar. On the up side, he's not a bad guy. And life can be fun if you like going to gigs with a load of clapped out 55-year-olds in denim jackets and cowboy boots.

The signs:

- He's still playing his LPs from the '70s.

- He speaks in a faux LA accent and uses words such as: 'babe', 'daddy o' and any other 'yoof' speak from yesteryear.

- He will serenade you with his old songs and give you the crooner look of desire. Don't laugh whatever you do!

- He will start sentences with, 'When I was young'.

How to handle
With an ego the size of Utah and as fragile as Venetian glass, the ARS can be a tricky animal. As long as you embrace the 'I'm still cool' spiel, you may find life chilling out in Marrakech with his ageing rock friends a real gas. Just be prepared for lots of conversations about when they met Mick and Bianca on tour and hazy reminiscing of the '60s.

The wealthy tycoon (WT)
Well, isn't he every woman's dream? Highly successful, dripping with power, charisma and a palatial mansion in St Barts, what's not to like? With his Armani suits, his yacht in the Med and his private helicopter, he has a lifestyle to be envied. Whether he is a wealthy millionaire with a string of high profile divorces under his belt, or a careering tycoon who spends his time bellowing into his mobile phone in the executive airport lounge, dating the WT is not all fun and lobster bisque. For a start, this is a man who never takes no for an answer. Even the likes of Richard Branson are at his beck and call. He is a super mate – the triple A personality – acquisitive, aggressive and accumulative, and along with the Rembrandts in the bathroom and the houses in Mustique, he wants you to be another of his possessions, for the time being anyway. By applying the business tactics of persuasion, coercion and determination, the WT is bound to sweep you off your feet whether you like it or not. But can you handle a man with a will of iron and the compassion of a third-world dictator? After all he didn't get where he is today by being kind and warm.

The signs:

- He enters the room with such confidence your heart will skip a beat and you will be putty in his hands.

- With a private suite at The Ritz, a box at Ascot and friends in high places, going on a date with WT is more like an adventure with the super rich.

- Like his zillions of employees and other 'yes' people, he will expect you to be on call, and that means at 11 pm when he has just arrived from New York and wants to see you for a late-night supper.

- He will expect things to be done his way. Cosseted and cocooned by years of yes people, he has forgotten that other people have opinions.

How to handle

Whatever you do, don't look or sound impressed. Even if you can just about afford a Pret a Manger sandwich doesn't mean you have to stand open mouthed when he turns up in his Testarossa with a Chanel ballgown on his arm. Spoilt and used to buying people's affections, the more aloof and unavailable you are, the more your stock will rise. The more you refuse to give into his whims, the more he will up the ante, and you may find yourself being taken to dinner on a private yacht in Belize. Enjoy!

HOW NOT TO BE SHORT-CHANGED ON THE LOVE FRONT

Ok, so most men will fall asleep on the sofa and watch footy all day long; some even spit in the street. That is all fine, albeit irritating. But be on the lookout for the red flags. These are the warning signs that the man you are seeing is a toxic rotter. And the problem with being a midlife singleton, is that often we are so happy to be with a man that we simply push the warning signs under the carpet.

Here are the red flags that mean gettouta there girl!

- He is unkind to you. He is a mean-spirited man who enjoys making you feel miserable.

- He puts you down in public. He is inadequate and jealous, and wants to chip away at your confidence.

- He never takes you out to restaurants or parties.. He is embarrassed about you or he is married. Dump now!

- He never just buys you a bunch of flowers, pays for a taxi or splashes out on you. He is so mean, he makes Scrooge look like Francis of Assisi.

- He disappears for days or even weeks on end. If you ask him where he's been, he will explode into a terrifying rage and tell you to stop nagging him.

- He always has to win. Whether he's playing ping-pong, having an argument or you are deciding where to go for dinner, it's his way or the highway. He is a power crazy, control freak.

- He has a roving eye and it isn't roving over you. His lights are on and he is still interested in other women.

- He always does what he wants and never makes any sacrifices for you. You are not a priority in his life and you never will be.

- When you tell him how you feel, he smoothes it over with empty platitudes and never changes. He is unwilling to bend and do what it takes to make you happy. And will always be the same.

- Everything has to be perfect. From the fluffiness of the towels in the bathroom to the cleanliness of the kitchen floor. His standards are impossible and you will run yourself ragged if you try to keep up with them.

- He shouts at the waiter and swears at people when he cuts them up in his car. He has anger issues and you'll soon find yourself in his line of fire.

- He goes on three-day sulk-athons and refuses to communicate with you. He is trying to grind you down and control you.

- He relentlessly tells you to do something he knows you don't want to do. He is not acknowledging your needs or you.

- You find yourself walking on eggshells and too scared to disagree with him. He is a bully and you are his victim.

- He says things like, 'If you loved me you would...' He is guilt-tripping you like a manipulative child.

Five things men find a turn on (that have nothing to do with boobs or blonde hair):

- Having a hearty appetite. Tucking into bangers and mash on a date is apparently more appealing than a bird-like creature who picks at her salad. (Something to do with passion for food equals passion in the bed.)

- Being adventurous. There is nothing more sexy than a woman who likes to unleash her dangerous side, whether it's a last-minute trip to the Maldives or a walk in the rain.

- Laughing at yourself. Men love it when women don't take themselves too seriously. It shows they have a playful side.

- Kindness. Contrary to popular belief, men are not impressed with ball-breaking Betsies. Most men want a woman who will nurture them and be kind to them and that includes giving them the last chocolate/the best side of the bed and the remote.

- Having a shower with you on a sweltering hot day.

Five things that turn men off:

- Clunky shoes and baggy clothes, and that includes harem pants and onesies!

- Tatoos. Unfeminine and remind them of a navvy.

- Gaggles of girls puffing away at the old smokes. Unless they have a 20-a-day habit, smoking is a mega turn off!

- Bad grooming habits. Especially bitten finger nails and old make-up.

- Swearing. Unless he's foreign and doesn't understand what you are saying, men hate it when a woman swears.

Should you ever get back with an ex? The short answer is, 'Like hell no'! After all, you've just spent six months or maybe a year crying him out of your system. You are over him. He is in the past and you are finally getting your life back on track.

So what happens if one day he sends you a text message asking you to meet up? What do you do? Do you delete asap? Or, do you dither? 'What could be the harm in a catch up and a coffee?' you say to yourself. After all, he wants you back. Feels good, eh? Suddenly you feel warm and loved once again. You start to play all the good times in your mind like a fuzzy romantic comedy in technicolor. 'Ok', you text back in a moment of nostalgic madness and you're off down the road of re-romancing. Have a look at the following before you get ready to meet him.

Five wrong reasons why people get back together:

- *Loneliness*: All those nights spent alone. Cooking spaghetti bolognese for one, waking up in the middle of the night and wishing he was next to you. Ask yourself whether it is him you miss or just the intimacy and closeness of another person.

- *Boredom*: You are sick and tired of making coq au vin for one. You can't bear to watch another episode of CSI without having someone to talk to. Again, boredom is down to you. If you are yawning at your own company, get out and about and start meeting new people.

- *He says he'll change*: Well don't all men promise the impossible. Often men are even worse at dealing with break-ups and believe that they can become kind and caring overnight if only you would give them the chance! It's probably wishful thinking. Real change means resolving the issues that broke you up in the first place. This takes time, effort and gold-star sacrifice. So don't hold your breath!

- *You are scared to go it alone*: Breaking up in the middle of your life can be tough and scary. What with 'will I meet someone ever again' paranoia and the fact that we have more wrinkles than corrugated iron, stepping out into the unknown is a bit like going to Mars. Suddenly the familiar seems so comforting. Make no mistake, all the conflicts that broke you up in the first place are bound to surface again.

- *You love the drama*: Could it be that you are a make-up, break-up queen? Are you more in love with the emotional roller coaster than you are with him? If you are one of those storm-out-of-the-house-never-to-see-you-again kinda gals, it's time to take stock. If your relationship is a constant to-ing and fro-ing – maybe you are both commitment phobes who are terrified of taking the relationship to the next level.

Here are some good reasons to re-hitch:

- You had a terrible argument and you've both been too proud to make the first move. You love each other really and you just need to back down. Both of you!

- You were both too busy. When commitments take over, our personal lives can suffer. Suddenly he misses your special Sunday lunch, ditto your birthday/anniversary and you are abroad when his mum comes over from Milwaukee. Before you know it, you are both brimming with resentments and recriminations. Don't let your arguments muddy the love waters. Take time out to sit down and discuss the problems. Be mature and don't play the blame game. Chances are he is as sorry as you are.

- You live in different countries. Geographical break-ups are common. After, if we don't get to see our loved ones all manner of strange thoughts can build up in our head. Does he love that cute secretary I saw on one of his facebook pages? The next minute you are on a plane and surprising him at his work. If long-distance romance split you up, take a break and ask yourself if he is the one for you. Call him and renegotiate.

Hooking up with exs of the distant past

What with Facebook, twitter and all those Friends Reunited sites, you can get in touch with every man you ever snogged/had a crush on/ dated. Whether you track them down and check out their status – stalking a married man is a no-go area – it can be fun/flirty or a way to make a whole new group of friends. If they are single and you like their profile picture why not have a chat. My own ex-journey started when Domenico my boyfriend from way back facebooked me. Dark and handsome, he was divorced and still looked as good as ever. We struck up a cyber friendship and soon felt the old feelings flooding back. When he invited me to spend time with him in his home town in Sicily, I booked a ticket the day after. Neither of us had any illusions of a long-term romance, but I had just broken up with my fiancée and our summer of love was just the tonic I needed. I returned, refreshed, revived and more determined than ever to make a fresh new start.

Having a flirtathon with a boyfriend from your teenage years can be exhilarating and fun. You are both adults, and as you haven't seen him in so long, it really is like going out with someone new only with the comfort of all those youthful memories.

Sex with the ex

You're stuck in the sexual Gobi and you haven't had so much as a hug in six months. Suddenly he is sexting (sex texting) you, sending you red roses and asking you to come round to his house? So is it time to slip on the stilettos or run for cover?

Don't do it if:

- You are using it as a way to get your ex back.

- You are lonely and you miss all the cuddles and late night kisses.

- You've had too much to drink.

- He's using it as a way to get you back in his arms.

- You want to get back at his current girlfriend.

Go for it if:

- You are totally over him and just want some extra-curricular fun.

- He is so great in bed, he is hard to resist, and you are over him.

- You want to use him to get back your mojo.

- He has turned into a friend with benefits.

- You know you will feel ok about it afterwards.

Dating down

A word on dating younger men.

Getting jiggy with the under 35s? What could be better you say? Whether you want Olympic sex or just a post-divorce pick-me-up, the younger man is a tonic with a six-pack and a full head of hair. Ok, so he doesn't know his way round the wine list and his 'yoof' speak may seem like a foreign language, but on the up side he has more energy than a Duracell battery and he will make you look and feel ten years younger.

Have a look at these pros and cons of dating down the age scale:

Pros
- They are the quickest way to shore up a middle-aged ego and more fun than a trip to a spa.

- They are enthusiastic and eager, which is more than can be said for the old codgers you have been dating recently.

- You may think you are a wrinkly old bag. All he sees is a wonderful goddess in designer suits and her own flat.

- He will text, email and flirt with you all day long.

- He thinks nothing of rushing out to buy you ice cream at four in the morning.

- He will introduce you to a whole new racy lifestyle.

- He is just the perfect rebound partner. Too young to be serious about, young enough to make you feel good.

Cons

- He will start his texts with 'waaaaaaasupppp' and do lots of smileys and other emoticons.

- After a while you'll need a daily dose of guarana and fresh papaya juice just to keep up with him.

- You will get bored of his friends and childish antics. That, or you'll sleep with them as well.

- Your friends will make fun of you (or be jealous of you).

- He may fall in love too soon and become a romantic cling-on.

- One day your middle-aged woman will rear its head, and you will yearn for an age-appropriate lifestyle. Your days of dancing till dawn are O.V.E.R.

~ Chapter Ten ~

FROM COCKTAILS TO COUPLEDOM

FINDING LOVE AGAIN

GOING COURTIN'

Ok, so the first/second date went well. He ticked some of your boxes; you laughed over a glass of bubbly, and discovered you both loved holidaying in southern Italy. All you can think about is his crooked smile and the way he makes your skin tingle all over. You may feel as if you've known him forever. You may want to rip off his shirt and take him home... Whoa girl! Steady on.

If you are adamant you want to jump into the sack before you can say, 'Pass me my undies', or you just want a roll in the hay (more of that later) then go for it! On the other hand, if you think he has potential as a love interest then it pays to be clever.

He may be incredibly handsome and you like him a lot. So what do you do next? After all, if you've just been through a hard break-up or come out of a long-term relationship, finding yourself back on the dating scene can seem a bit overwhelming and confusing. Do you sleep with him on the third date – as they say in Sex and the City? Do you lay down the law and tell him you want a ring on your finger by the end of the year? Or, do you say nothing, smile sweetly and play hard to get?

How to drive the love bus

Think about it. One minute you're kissing on the sofa, the next you're naked and swinging from the chandelier. It's so easy to get swept away by passion, especially if you are very attracted to someone. And particularly if there have been large glasses of wine involved and lots of dancing to Abba. Whatever you do, don't make the rookie mistake of confusing lust for intimacy. Just because you really like someone, shared intimate moments with them as you walked hand in hand in the park, doesn't mean that you are an item. In other words, if you sleep with someone before you know where you are with each other, then you could be setting yourself up for a fall.

Questions such as 'Are we on the same relationship page?' 'Does he like me enough?' 'Will he stick around?' should all be answered before you spend the night with him. You may think it's a relationship.

He may think it's something casual, and so much so that if you're sleeping together and he disappears for a weekend with the boys and doesn't phone you, you may feel aggrieved. You may even pull a hissy fit and slam the phone down. He'll think, 'Whoa! too much pressure', and may put you in the bunny boiler category. And that will be it.

The truth is men don't think that having sex means that they are in a relationship. Women often do. And just because he's middle aged doesn't mean he wants commitment with you. Indeed, think about it. If he's just come out of a marriage, he may feel like sowing his wild oats all over again. Don't be an oat! While making him wait doesn't guarantee life-long happiness, or that he will carve your name into his chest, it will make the whole thing a lot more romantic and keep you in the driving seat. Trust me, in today's modern dating world, where the traditional rules have been swept away, it pays to have your own dating template.

Here are some of the dating strategies that will keep him wanting more:

Don't get jiggy with it: If you think your date has long-term prospects, then whatever you do don't have a sleepover with him just yet. After all, if you have shown him your best Hollywood kiss, then he knows you're attracted to him, which is enough for the time being. It may seem natural to progress to the next stage and he may be putting on the 'if you really liked me you would sleep with me', pressure, but no woman will ever regret waiting. Besides, a man will jump through burning hoops and swim shark-infested waters all on a promise.

Keep him guessing: Don't let him know how you feel about him too soon. Telling him you really love being in his company on date three is a big mistake in dating terms. If you keep your feelings under wraps he'll have to make more of an effort to find out what you are thinking, and it will focus his emotions on you.

Be friendly to everyone: While overt flirting with other men will just make him resent you, you do want him to see you as a warm friendly person. Laugh a lot and turn up the heat. Being popular is always a plus sign in a future mate.

Don't answer all his calls: Let the answer phone pick up once in a while. Not knowing what you are doing all the time will pique his interest and increase his ardour.

Don't be too available: Ditto, don't say you're free for the rest of the month so pick a date! Even if your diary is about as blank as a white sheet of paper, he doesn't have to know that, does he? Tell him you are seeing friends (again not too much information) have an early night and relax in the knowledge that you've got him going!

Dress to kill and a*ct like a nun*: Men are programmed to want to get you into bed. During the courtship phase, if you have kept him at bay, he'll be fantasising like Billio. Give him something to fantasise about, by dressing to thrill. By wearing your sexiest outfits (nothing too re-vealing or else you'll just look desperate), you'll arouse his desires without fulfilling them.

Whoa steady boy!

There are ways to keep a man at bay without hurting his pride. Wait-ing until he lunges at you with a clumsy grope and telling him to 'be-have himself', will only confuse him and dent his ego. You need to let him know where you both stand before he tries to cop a handful. So, how do you let him down gently? When he starts to get an acute case of wandering hand trouble, lean in and smile. Tell him you are having a great time, and that it would be much nicer to wait until you got to know each other better before moving on to the next stage. Let him know by your body language how much you like him. There is nothing wrong with sensuous kissing, but don't give him anymore. That way he is on a promise and will be putting in overtime to impress you.

Which brings me to the million-dollar question: how long should I make him wait? That is entirely up to you. However as a rough guide, I would always say stick to the two-to-three-month rule. 'So long?' you say. Well eight to twelve weeks will give you time to get to know each other better and to see if you care for each other. If he is showing all the positive signs: if he is kind, loyal and you feel that he appreciates you, then maybe it's time to take the plunge. Don't feel pressured though. There's nothing wrong with keeping him dangling for six months if that's how you feel. If he really likes you, then it shouldn't matter to him. If it does matter, then he wasn't that interested in the first place.

Which brings me to my next point. Keep the dating period fun and light hearted. You don't need to get all serious and heavy just because you won't let him unzip your dress. Use humour and a coquettish smile as you wriggle free, then make him an extra strong gin and tonic. Being sexy but firm will go a long way to keeping the tension without making it feel tense and awkward.

Extreme dating

Extreme dating is about going out with several different men at once. Enjoying à la carte dining and long walks in the countryside with Tom, Dick and Harry is a great way to fill a weekend and make you feel a million dollars. Getting attention and flattery from more than one man is one of the best ways to shore up a flagging midlife ego. If you aren't sleeping with any of them, then you aren't breaking any intimate bond and more importantly you aren't compromising how you feel.

And there's the nub. The key to extreme dating is to keep things casual. This is the time to get to know prospective boyfriends and see if they are on the same emotional/taste/value page. And it's much easier to find these things out if you aren't complicating things with sex. And, of course, there is the question of time, which for the midlife dater is at a premium. You don't want to be spending months on one guy only to find out that he loves recycled furniture and wants to live in an eco hut, while you are a full-on city girl with a taste in minimal decor. Multi-dating gives you the opportunity to maximise your time and get to know what you really want.

Six rules of text-iquette

In the world of digi-romance there are many different ways to keep in contact with your dates. From emails and facebook to texting, keeping tabs on the men in your life is a full-time job. Before you start tapping loving missives to 'your intended', here are some tips to keep your texting savvy.

Don't be the first to text him: Just because texting is so casual it still falls under the same rules as any other forms of communication, which in the early stages of a courtship should be initiated by him. After all, where is the chase if you show him your hand after the first date and send him a flurry of texts with lots of smiley emoticons.

Learn to text volley: In other words, how long do you wait before you ping back a text? My rule of thumb is no less than fifteen minutes. It shows that you are enthusiastic but you may be busy. If he lobs back a sweet text immediately, you can relax your rule. If he wants to play games and leaves it an hour, double it, he will get the message.

Don't be the last one to text: If you are having a bit of texting banter, try to ask a question at the end of each one, that way you are guaranteed a text back.

Don't be a sext (sex texting) girl: Getting involved in sending him smutty jokes may be fun, but it could back fire – he will think you are up for it and put all his energy into getting you into bed. If he sends you a pic of his bare torso (as a date did to me) or tells you what he wants to do to you, don't get angry. The trick is to play the lady card. Point out that that kind of behaviour is not very gentlemanly. If he likes you he will change tack and maybe even turn up with a dozen red roses the next time he sees you – mine did!

Don't over think the texts: When I was dating, I'd put more effort into one text to him than an entire day's work. He won't be doing the same and he certainly won't be picking your text apart for hidden meanings (it's a girl thing). Ditto how many kisses at the end of the text. Rule of thumb: one kiss is casual, two says I like you, three should be held back till after the big night.

Don't leave your phone unattended: If you are multi dating, you would be wise to keep your phone hidden from view and on silent. You don't want to cause suspicion by avoiding 'certain' calls or disappearing off to the loo only to find the date that you are currently with has answered your phone.

The hook-up

While you are looking for love, does that mean you have to spend time in the sexual Gobi – aka no sex? Is there anything to stop you having the occasional hook up (casual sex)? After all, if the chemistry is there, great sex can be liberating, wild and make you feel attractive and sexy again. It can give you that post-coital glow and most probably will make you smile for 24 hours straight.

Of course there are rules to the midlife hook-up. Sex complicates things unless you know what you're doing.

My rules of hook-up go like this:

Don't have casual sex with anyone you think has serious potential: If you jump into bed with the gorgeous guy that you've been fantasising about for ages, the one you have mentally been walking down the aisle with, then put the waiting plan into action.

Don't turn to sex to get that loved-up feeling: if you have sex when you really want the post-coital cuddle and smooch, then a hook up is the wrong way to go. Casual sex is about just that, sex. It can be exciting, make you feel alive and unleash your inner scarlet woman. You can go fifty or even sixty shades of grey. You can do things you never thought imaginable, but no matter how great and how good you feel, sex cannot take the place of true intimacy. If you have slept with him on the first date, don't expect him to shower you with affection the morning after. Think of it this way: If you can't handle the morning coffee with an impersonal chat followed by a casual peck on the cheek then it pays to wait for Mr Hope He's Right, rather than go the wild route.

Get what you want from it: Great sex is about rekindling your inner fire and making you feel attractive again. It's a sort of refuelling station to keep you tanked up with fuzzy pheromones! Keep it physical and don't contact him. If he calls you and wants to meet up again, then that's your call. If you think you can keep it light and not get too emotionally involved then go to dinner, see a movie and throw caution to the wind. However, be careful. I know a lot of women who have started down the 'fuck buddy' route and ended up with egg on their face. In other words, as soon as you start to feel that he's yours, or that you miss him, either have 'the conversation' or quit while you're ahead.

The booty call: Should you drop everything you are doing and rush round to his house if he gives you the booty call, aka the late-night call for sex? If you feel like it, and know you can handle the repercussions, then why not? If you want to exercise a little more control, then tell him you're busy and rearrange to suit your schedule – after all you are a busy girl.

THE ONE

So you've dated, danced and played the romantic hokey cokey with several romantic prospects. After a whirlwind of glorious dating not only do you feel you have turned the dating corner, you have finally met someone you want to take things further with.

It doesn't matter how successful/secure or how great you feel: If there is one thing to get a middlie running for the hills and wailing 'help' at the top of her voice, it's getting naked for the first time. Thoughts such as, 'What will he think of me?' And, 'Do I have more wobbly bits than a midlife telly tubby?' may hurtle through your mind to give you a big dose of midlife dating anxiety.

After a break-up, we can all feel insecure about the prospect of life between the sheets with someone new. We may have lost the confidence we once had when we were young – middle age back fat, love handles and sprouting grey hairs are not going to make us feel like doing the dance of the seven veils with nipple tassels! Then there are the years spent in comfy coupledom and being accepted for who we are, wobbly bits and all. So much so, that the prospect of getting naked and risking re-appraisal can send us into a spiral of will-he-reject-me panic.

So, how do you get over the pre-pounce panic? We may not be 20-something anymore, but then neither is he. We all desire intimate touch and closeness, and he is hardly going to be looking you over with a magnifying glass. And, if he is, do you really want to date him? After all, he's bound to have a bit of a paunch/hint of a man boob or even stick-on chest hairs. Besides, he's probably just so grateful that you've finally given in! So don't think you have to morph into a bikini-fit 40-something just because you are showing off your curves for the first time.

HOW TO BE AT PEACE WITH YOUR SHAPE

Being sexy is not about having a flat stomach and the legs of a stick insect. Just because the red carpet seems to have spawned a legion of perfect celebrities with bodies the size of five-year-olds, is not the benchmark of sex appeal. How we act, move and feel are just as important as buff bottoms and perfect arms.

Here are five ways to get some midlife sex appeal:

Feel good, look good: How we feel about ourselves and how we act, are closely bound together. If you feel good about yourself then your confidence will shine through. Yeah right, you say. Easier said than done when you have orange peel stuck to your thighs and your batwings are being used as wind turbines by the electricity board. Learning to love your body is the first step to getting bedroom confidence.

Don't compare yourself to others: Just because the media is fixated with perfect bodies doesn't mean that you have to be. There will always be someone, younger, prettier, slimmer or richer than you are. If you start down the road of who's-better-than-me you'll end up with an ulcer!

Focus on your best bits: Every woman has the bits she hates. Whether it's your ankles, blancmange-like stomach or shoulders like a wrestler, none of us are perfect. Instead of scrutinising your slightly plump thighs, why not concentrate on your good bits. We all have something that is fabulous. It could be almond-shaped eyes, breasts men want to bury their heads in, or legs that go on forever. Whatever it is, it's your USP (unique selling point). Play it up and enjoy it. Focusing on what is good about yourself will make you feel happier, sexier and more confident.

Stop dwelling on what you looked like at 30: Getting out the old photos and going down good-bod-memory-lane is so not a good idea. So, you had eyes like limpid pools of blue water, your cheeks were plump and firm. Great. Let the past stay where it is – in the past. It's time to focus on the here and now.

Walk with va va voom: The next time you go for a walk, whether in the park or to the shops, why not try to up the ante? Instead of just marching like a woman on a mission, slow down and inject a bit of va va voom. Let your hips sway from side to side and start thinking sexy thoughts. Take note of any shift in feeling, and the change in movement. If you start to act more like Marilyn Monroe than your usual self, then hold onto that feeling and take it home with you.

Watch a porno movie: 'Whaaat?' You screech as you throw the book down. Hang on a minute. When I came out of a relationship, I really thought I was out of practice. After years of chugging along with a bed routine that involved a bit of missionary with the occasional doggy-style thrown in, I'd got into a sex rut. It wasn't until I broke up with my fiancée that I woke up and smelt the *Kama Sutra*. A friend urged me to take some tips from the porn stars and sex guides, and soon I was taking notes. Just watching how the porn stars move can give you some good tips if you feel a bit rusty.

Wear sexy underwear: That doesn't mean you have to go the Victoria's Secret route and greet him with suspenders and crotchless knickers. Investing in pretty, sexy underwear will not only make you feel better and more confident, it will show him that you care enough to make an effort.

Take pride in your appearance: While making a big deal of 'the date', could cause you more anxiety than it's worth, keeping yourself preened and buffed for the moment you feel is right, means you'll always be at your fighting best. Waxed, trimmed and perfumed is a good way to look in the run up to the big night.

Bedroom pitfalls

After years of being with the same guy, some of us can get a bit lazy on the preening front. You may have got used to slipping into the winceyette nightdress or a pair of old jim jams and padding around the house in Mickey Mouse slippers. When it comes to being bedroom savvy, there are some things you should avoid.

Don't:

Ask him if your bottom looks big in this: Chances are he never thought about it until you pointed towards your derrière and gave him a run down on the way you hate the droop. Really, men don't fixate on our bits as much as we do. They are just thankful to be getting some.

Keep the lights off: Unless you are really nervous and can't face showing yourself, shedding a little light on the situation will keep his interest. Men like to see what they're getting.

Walk around the house naked: He may have seen you naked in bed, you may have swapped bodily fluids and you may think you are now one. I always think it pays to rekindle the mystery when you get up to make a post-coital Martini/coffee. Pulling on some boy shorts and a camisole or a pretty négligée not only looks sexy, it will excite his imagination all over again.

Wear the same old underwear: Take a friend and buy some really sexy underwear. Men are visual creatures and the sight of you in a pink silken teddy is going to get his pulse racing faster than jumping out of an aeroplane.

So how do you know if he is in it for the long-term, or if you're just another notch on his middle class bedstead?

There you are snuggled up in bed watching your favourite black-

and-white film. You get on really well and you love being in his company. The trouble is you've been dating him for several months now and you haven't even met his children, he never spends the weekend with you and he is always cancelling your plans. So, before you go and invest more time in him, here are some ways to know if he is a catch or a cad.

He's in it for the long term if:

- He still kisses you when you have foul morning breath.

- He sacrifices things/plans for you. He is prioritising the relationship because it is important to him.

- He introduces you to his family/children/colleagues.

- He is jealous when other men talk to you.

- He takes you on a round-the-world trip with him.

- He is decorating his country cottage the way you like it.

- You make decisions together.

It's casual if:

- He never invites you to his weekend cottage.

- He looks at other women.

- He always phones you late at night to come over (it's a booty call).

- He doesn't want to spend time with your family.

- He doesn't introduce you to his children.

- You never spend the night at his place (he's probably married).

Bad sex

A word about bad sex. With all the baggage and emotions that can be flying around, it could happen to anyone. After all, if you have waited and built up your expectations, he or you may feel the pressure is on. If you hit the sack and instead of angels flying overhead it is more like flicking through the yellow pages and falling asleep, then don't worry, bad sex doesn't necessarily mean bad in bed. There are several reasons for poor performance.

Either:

- You both freaked a bit and lost your nerve.

- You drank too much and fell asleep just as he was getting to the good bit.

- His ex-wife walked in.

- He or you are worried about work/children.

- You like him so much you got an attack of 'am I good enough?' panic. Or else, he did.

Whatever the reason, don't avoid the issue. Talk about it, but keep it light. You might say, 'Wow I think we were a bit nervous', and then show him that it's not important to you. When it comes to action between the sheets, men care a lot more than women how they come across. Reassure him without denting his fragile ego. Pour a drink, change the subject and give him a loving kiss.

THE COUPLES CURVE

So, now you've been together for several months. You've got past the stage where you greet him with full make-up, fuck-me heels and a come-hither smile. You don't feel that every conversation is a full-on flirt-athon with witty banter and lots of double entendre, and you enjoy just spending time with him in a state of cosy comfort. You even have your own drawer at his place and cordon-bleu cooking has taken the place of cocktails and cabs at three in the morning.

This is the time when:

- Instead of wanting to rip his clothes off every time you see him, you get a warm, fuzzy feeling of closeness.

- People start inviting you out as a couple.

- It doesn't feel strange to stay in on a Friday night and watch Mad Men.

- He would rather spend time with you than with his mates.

- You know how he takes his coffee/likes his eggs and his favourite slap-up meal.

- You can get annoyed when he doesn't call without feeling like a cling-on.

- Your friends ask how he is whenever they call.

- You are building trust and intimacy.

At the early stages of coupledom not only will you be feeling that wonderful sense of togetherness and closeness, chances are the ghosts of the relationship past can rear their ugly head. If you have been hurt in the last relationship, you may find it difficult to trust someone again. Allowing yourself to believe in a new partner can be difficult and feel scary. Take it one step at a time. Let him do nice things for you and if you find that things are going too quickly or becoming too intense, tell him you adore him but could he slow it down a little? And whatever you do, don't cry during sex. Sex can unleash powerful feelings, especially in women. So, be careful if you suddenly feel overwhelmed with emotion just as he's getting on down. Try to hold back the floodgates until after. Rush off to the bathroom, cry a river, and when you return red and flushed he'll think it's for the right reason.

At some stage, if things are going well, you will naturally want to have the: 'What kind of relationship do we want' conversation. You may want to proceed to the rules of engagement and he may prefer to co-habit. You owe it to each other to be honest about where things are going. Second-time around relationships have far more variables than the meet-and-marry type of your 20s and 30s. Some men and women are so scared of failing the second time around that they are completely marriage shy. It pays to know who you are dealing with.

Whatever relationship you are in, congratulations. You made it. Good luck and be happy.

£12.99